THE SECRET
OF SUCCESS
IN THE
CHRISTIAN
LIFE

THE SECRET OF SUCCESS IN THE CHRISTIAN LIFE

D. L. MOODY

MOODY PRESS
CHICAGO

© 2001 by
MOODY BIBLE INSTUTUTE

Originally published as
Secret Power
© 1908 by Fleming H. Revell

Library of Congress Cataloging-in-Publication Data

Moody, Dwight Lyman, 1837–1899
    [Secret power]
    The secret of success in the Christian life / D.L. Moody.
        p. cm.
    Originally published: The secret power. Chicago: F.H. Revell, 1908.
    ISBN 0-8024-5217-5
        1. Holy Spirit. 2. Baptism in the Holy Spirit. 3. Christian life.
        I. Title

BT122 .M58 2001
234'.13—dc21

                                                            2001031268

1 3 5 7 9 10 8 6 4 2

Printed in the United States of America

CONTENTS

Note to Our Readers   7

1. Secret Power: Its Source   9

2. Secret Power: "In" and "Upon"   33

3. Witnessing in Power   59

4. Power in Operation   81

5. Hindered Power   107

NOTE TO OUR READERS

The ultimate impact of any book can be measured by how well the author communicates on a particular subject. The accuracy of the message and its relevance to the reader are also critical elements that distinguish a select group of books that are available. Most important, those books that build on the foundation of the Bible, with an overriding goal of glorifying God, are the ones that will stand the test of time.

This group of books, taken from the archives of Moody Press, meet those criteria. They are clear in their presentation and easy to read and apply to your life. At the same time, they do not compromise on substance, while presenting strong arguments that remain relevant to today's reader.

The authors write with elegance and conviction; their passion will inspire you. We have chosen to use the New King James Version of the Bible, which maintains the beauty and grace of the original King James Version while being highly readable in today's language.

This series of books is part of our Life Essentials™ line of products because the books fit so well with Life Essentials' objective: to help the readers stay focused on the essentials of life by keeping God at the center of all they do, grounding them in those truths that build their faith and obedience to the triune God.

We pray that these books will bless and help you in your walk of faith, just as they have done for followers of Jesus Christ in past generations.

THE PUBLISHER

CHAPTER ONE

SECRET POWER: ITS SOURCE

SOMEONE UNKNOWN ONCE SAID, "Without the soul, divinely quickened and inspired, the observances of the grandest ritualism are as worthless as the motions of a galvanized corpse." I quote this sentence as it leads me at once to the subject under consideration. What is this quickening and inspiration? What is this power needed for success in the Christian life? From whence its source?

I reply: "The Holy Spirit of God." This is the "secret" power. I am a full believer in The Apostles' Creed, and therefore say, "I believe in the Holy Ghost."

A writer has pointedly asked: "What are our souls without His grace? As dead as the branch in which the sap does not circulate. What is the church without Him? As parched and barren as the fields without the dew and rain of heaven."

There has been much inquiry of late on the subject of the Holy Spirit. In this and other lands, thousands of persons have been giving attention to the study of this grand theme. I hope it will lead us all to pray for a greater manifestation of His power upon the whole church of God. How much we have dishonored Him in the past! How ignorant of His grace and love and presence we have been! True, we have heard of Him and read of Him, but we have had little intelligent knowledge of His attributes, His offices, and His relations to us. I fear He has not been to many professed Christians an actual existence, nor is He known to them as a personality of the Godhead.

The first work of the Spirit is to give life—spiritual life. He gives it and He sustains it. If there is no life, there can be no power; Solomon says: "A living dog is better than a dead lion" (Ecclesiastes 9:4). When the Spirit imparts this life, He does not leave us to droop and die, but constantly fans the flame. He is ever with us. Surely we ought not to be ignorant of His power and His work.

IDENTITY AND PERSONALITY

In 1 John 5:7, we read: "There are three that bear witness in heaven: the Father, the Word, and the Holy Spirit; and these three are one." By the Father is meant the first Person; Christ, the Word, is the second; and the Holy Spirit, perfectly fulfilling His own office and work in union with the Father and the Son, is the third. I find clearly presented in my Bible that the one God who demands my love, service, and worship has there revealed Himself, and that each of those three names of Father, Son, and Holy Spirit has personality attached to it.

Therefore we find some things ascribed to God as Father, some to God as Savior, and some to God as Comforter and Teacher. It has been remarked that the Father plans, the Son executes, and the Holy Spirit applies. But I also believe they plan and work together.

The distinction of *persons* is often noted in Scripture. In Matthew 3:16–17, we find Jesus submitting to baptism, the *Spirit* descending upon Him, while the *Father's* voice of approval is heard, saying: "This is My beloved Son, in whom I am well pleased." Again, in John 14:16, we read: "I [that is, Jesus] will pray the Father, and He will give you another Helper." Also in Ephesians 2:18, "Through Him [that is, Christ Jesus] we both [Jews and Gentiles] have access by one Spirit to the Father." Thus we are taught the distinction of persons in the Godhead and their inseparable union. From these and other Scriptures also, we learn the identity and actual existence of the Holy Spirit.

If you ask do I *understand* what is thus revealed in Scripture, I say no. But my faith bows down before the inspired Word and I unhesitatingly believe the great

11

things of God when even reason is blinded and the intellect confused.

PRESENCE AND POWER

In addition to the teaching of God's Word, the Holy Spirit in His gracious work in the soul declares His own presence. Through His agency we are "born again," and through His indwelling we possess superhuman power. Science, falsely so-called, when arrayed against the existence and presence of the Spirit of God with His people, only exposes its own folly to the contempt of those who have become new creatures in Christ Jesus. The Holy Spirit who inspired prophets and qualified apostles continues to animate, guide, and comfort all true believers. To the actual Christian, the personality of the Holy Spirit is more real than any theory science has to offer, for so-called science is but calculation based on human observation, and is constantly changing its inferences. But the existence of the Holy Spirit is to the child of God a matter of Scripture revelation and of actual experience.

Some skeptics assert that there is no other vital energy in the world but physical force, while contrary to their assertions thousands and tens of thousands, who cannot possibly be deceived, have been brought into spiritual life by a power neither spiritual nor mental. Men who were dead in sins—drunkards who lost their will, blasphemers who lost their purity, libertines sunk in beastliness, infidels who published their shame to the world—have in numberless instances become the subjects of the Spirit's power, and are now walking in the true nobility of Christian manhood, separated by an infinite distance from their former life.

Let others reject, if they will, at their own peril, this imperishable truth. I believe that divine, miraculous creative power resides in the Holy Spirit. Above and beyond all natural law, yet in harmony with it, creation, providence, the divine government, and the upbuilding of the church of God are presided over by the Spirit of God. His ministration is the ministration of life more glorious than the ministration of law (2 Corinthians 3:6–10). And like the eternal Son, the eternal Spirit, having life in Himself, is working out all things after the counsel of His own will and for the everlasting glory of the triune Godhead.

The Holy Spirit has all the qualities belonging to a person: the power to understand, to will, to do, to call, to feel, and to love. This cannot be said of a mere influence. He possesses attributes and qualities that can be ascribed only to a person, as acts and deeds are performed by Him that cannot be performed by a machine, an influence, or a result.

AGENT AND INSTRUMENT

The Holy Spirit is closely identified with the words of the Lord Jesus. "It is the Spirit who gives life; the flesh profits nothing. The words that I speak to you are spirit, and they are life" (John 6:63). The

Gospel proclamation cannot be divorced from the Holy Spirit. Unless He attend the Word in power, vain will be the attempt in preaching it. Human eloquence or persuasiveness of speech are the mere trappings of the dead, if the living Spirit be absent. The prophet may preach to the bones in the valley, but it must be the breath from heaven that will cause the slain to live.

In 1 Peter 3 it reads, "For Christ also suffered once for all sins, the just for the unjust, that He might bring us to God, being put to death in the flesh but made alive by the Spirit" (v. 18). Here we see that Christ was raised up from the grave by this same Spirit, and the power exercised to raise Christ's dead body must raise our dead souls and quicken them. No other power on earth can quicken a dead soul, but the same power that raised the body of Jesus Christ out of Joseph's sepulchre.

If we want that power to quicken our friends who are dead in sin, we must look to God the Spirit, and not be looking to man to do it. If we look alone to ministers, if we look alone to Christ's disciples to do this work, we shall be disappointed; but if we look to the Spirit of God and expect it to come from Him and Him alone, then we shall honor the Spirit, and the Spirit will do His work.

THE SECRET OF EFFICIENCY

I cannot help but believe there are many Christians who want to be more efficient in the Lord's service, and the object of this book is to take up this subject of the Holy Spirit, that they may see from whom to expect this power.

In the teaching of Christ, in His last words recorded in Matthew, we find that the Son and the Holy Spirit are equal with the Father. "Go therefore and make disciples of all the nations, baptizing them in the name of the Father and of the Son and of the Holy Spirit." Here the Son and the Holy Spirit are one with Him: "baptizing them in the name of the Father, and of the Son, and of the Holy Spirit" (28:19).

Christ was now handing His commission over to His apostles. He was going to leave them. His work on earth was finished, and He was now just about ready to take His seat at the right hand of God, and He spoke unto them and said: "All authority has been given to Me in heaven and on earth" (28:18). All authority; so then, He had full authority. If Christ was mere man, as some people try to make out, it would have been blasphemy for Him to have commanded the disciples to go and baptize all nations in the name of the Father, and in His own name, and that of the Holy Spirit, making Himself equal with the Father.

There are three things: *All authority* has been given to Me; go, *teach all* nations. Teach them what? To *observe* all things. There are a great many people now that are willing to observe what they like about Christ, but the things that they don't like they just dismiss and turn away from. But His commission to His disciples was, "Go . . . teaching them to observe all things that I have commanded you." And what right has a messenger who has been sent of God to change the message? If I had sent a servant to deliver a message, and the servant thought the message didn't sound exactly right—a little harsh—and that servant went and changed the message, I should change servants very quickly; he could not serve me any longer. And when a minister or a messenger of Christ begins to change the message because he thinks it is not exactly what it ought to be, and thinks he is wiser than God, God just dismisses that man. They haven't taught "all things." They have left out some of the things that Christ has commanded us to teach, because they didn't correspond with man's reason.

We have to take the Word of God just as it is; and if we are going to take it, we have no authority to take out just what we like, what we think is appropriate, and let dark reason be our guide. It is the work of the Spirit to impress the heart and seal the preached Word. His office is to take of the things of Christ and reveal them to us.

Some people have the idea that this is the only dispensation of the Holy Spirit, that He didn't work until Christ was glorified. But Simeon felt the Holy Spirit when he went into the temple. In 2 Peter 1:21, we read: "Holy men of God spoke as they were moved by the Holy Spirit." We find the same Spirit in Genesis as is seen in Revelation. The same Spirit who guided the hand that wrote Exodus inspired also the Epistles, and we find the same Spirit speaking from one end of the Bible to the other. So holy men in all ages have spoken as they were moved by the Holy Spirit.

HIS PERSONALITY

I was a Christian a long time before I found out that the Holy Spirit was a person. Now this is something a great many don't seem to understand, but if you will just take up the Bible and see what Christ had to say about the Holy Spirit, you will find that He always spoke of Him as a person—never spoke of Him as an influence. Some people have the idea that the Holy Spirit is an attribute of God, just like mercy— just an influence coming from God. But we find in John 14:16 these words: "And I will pray the Father, and He will give you another Helper, that *He* may abide with you forever" (italics added). And in the next verse Jesus described that Helper: "the Spirit of truth, whom the world cannot receive, because it neither sees Him nor knows Him; but you know Him, for He dwells with you and will be in you." Again, in verse 26: "But the Helper, the Holy Spirit, whom the Father will send in My name, He will teach you all things, and bring to your remembrance all things that I said to you."

Observe the pronouns "He" and "Him." Whenever Christ spoke of the Holy Spirit, He spoke of Him as a

17

person, not a mere influence. If we want to honor the Holy Spirit, let us bear in mind that He is one of the Trinity, a personality in the Godhead.

THE RESERVOIR OF LOVE

We read that the fruit of the Spirit is love. God is love, Christ is love, and we should not be surprised to read about the love of the Spirit. What a blessed attribute is this. May I call it the dome of the temple of the graces? Better still, it is the crown of crowns worn by the Triune God. Human love is a natural emotion that flows forth towards the object of our affections. But divine love is as high above human love as the heaven is above the earth.

The natural man is of the earth, earthy, and however pure his love may be, it is weak and imperfect at best. But the love of God is perfect and entire, wanting nothing. It is as a mighty ocean in its greatness, dwelling with and flowing from the eternal Spirit.

In Romans 5:5, we read: "Now hope does not disappoint, because the love of God has been poured out in our hearts by the Holy Spirit who was given to us." Now if we are coworkers with God, there is one thing we must possess, and that is love. A man may be a very successful lawyer and have no love for his clients, and yet get on very well. A man may be a very successful physician and have no love for his patients, and yet be a very good physician. A man may be a very successful merchant and have no love for his customers, and yet he may do a good business and succeed. But no man can be a coworker with God without love. If our service is mere profession on our part, the quicker we renounce it the better. If a man takes up God's work as he would take up any profession, the sooner he gets out of it the better.

We cannot work for God without love. It is the only tree that can produce fruit on this sin-cursed earth, that is acceptable to God. If I have no love for God nor for my fellow man, then I cannot work acceptably. I am like sounding brass and a clanging cymbal. We are told that "the love of God has been poured out in our hearts by the Holy Spirit." Now, if we have had that love shed abroad in our hearts, we are ready for God's service; if we have not, we are not ready. It is so easy to reach a man when you love him; all barriers are broken down and swept away.

Paul, when writing to Titus (2:2), told him to be sound in faith, in love, and in patience. Now in this age, ever since I can remember, the church has been very jealous about men being unsound in the faith. If a man becomes unsound in the faith, those in the church draw their ecclesiastical sword and cut at him; but he may be ever so unsound in love, and they don't say anything. He may be ever so defective in patience; he may be irritable and fretful all the time, but they never deal with him. Now the Bible teaches us that we are not only to be sound in the faith, but in love and patience. I believe God cannot use many of His servants because they are full of irritability and impatience; they are fretting all the time, from morning until night. God cannot use them; their mouths are sealed; they cannot speak for Jesus Christ, and if they have not love, they cannot work for God.

I do not mean love for those that love me; it does not take grace to do that; the rudest pagan in the world can do that; the greatest heathen who ever lived can do that; the vilest man who ever walked the earth can do that. It doesn't take any grace at all. I did that before I ever became a Christian.

Love begets love; hatred begets hatred. If I know that a man loves me first, I know my love will be going out toward him. Suppose a man comes to me, saying, "Mr. Moody, a certain man told me today that he thought you were the meanest man living." Well, if I didn't have a good deal of the grace of God in my heart, then I know that hard feelings would spring up in my heart against that man, and it would not be long before I would be talking against him. Hatred begets hatred. But suppose a man comes to me and says, "Mr. Moody, do you know that such a man that I met today says that he thinks a great deal of you?" Though I may never have heard of him, there would be love springing up in my heart.

Love begets love; we know that; but it takes the grace of God to love the man who lies about me, the man who is trying to tear down my character. You may hate the sin he has committed; there is a difference between the sin and the sinner. You may hate the one with a perfect hatred, but you must love the sinner. You cannot otherwise do him any good.

Now you know the first impulse of a young convert is to love. Do you remember the day you were converted? Was not your heart full of sweet peace and love?

THE RIGHT OVERFLOW

I remember the morning I came out of my room after I had first trusted Christ, and I thought the old sun shone a good deal brighter than it ever had before; I thought that the sun was just smiling upon me, and I walked out upon Boston Common, and I heard the birds in the trees, and I thought that they were all singing a song for me. Do you know I fell in love with the birds? I never cared for them before; it seemed to me that I was in love with all creation. I had not a bitter feeling against any man, and I was ready to take all men to my heart. If a man has not the love of God poured out in his heart, he has never been regenerated. If you hear a person get up in prayer meeting, and he begins to speak and find fault with everybody, you may know that his is not a genuine conversion; that it is counterfeit. It has not the right ring, because the impulse of a converted soul is to love, and not to be getting up and complaining of everyone else, and finding fault.

Now it is hard for us to live in the right atmosphere all the time. Someone comes along and treats

21

us wrongly, perhaps we hate him. We have not attended to the means of grace and kept feeding on the Word of God as we ought; a root of bitterness springs up in our hearts. Perhaps we are not aware of it, but it has come up in our hearts; then we are not qualified to work for God. The love of God is not pouring forth in our hearts as it ought to be by the Holy Spirit. But the work of the Holy Spirit is to impart love.

Paul could say, "Christ's love compels us" (2 Corinthians 5:14). He could not help going from town to town and preaching the Gospel. Jeremiah at one time said: "I will speak no more in the Lord's name; I have suffered enough; these people don't like God's Word." They lived in a wicked day, as we do now. Infidels were creeping up all around him, who said the Word of God was not true. Jeremiah had stood like a wall of fire, confronting them, and he boldly proclaimed that the Word of God was true. At last they put him in prison, and he said: "I will keep still; it has cost me too much."

But a little while after, you know he could not keep still. His bones caught fire; he had to speak. And when we are so full of the love of God that we are compelled to work for God, then God blesses us. If our work is driven by the lash, without any true motive power, it will come to naught.

Now the question comes up, Have we the love of God shed abroad in our hearts, and are we holding the truth in love? Some people hold the truth, but in such a cold, stern way that it will do no good. Other people want to love everything, and so they give up much of the truth; but we are to hold the truth in love; we are to hold the truth even if we lose all, but we are to hold it in love, and if we do that, the Lord will bless us.

THE TRIUMPH OF LOVE

A good many people are trying to get this love; they are trying to produce it of themselves. But therein all fail. The love implanted deep in our new nature will be spontaneous. I don't have to learn to love my children. I cannot help loving them. Some time ago in an inquiry meeting, a young miss told me that it was very hard for her to love God. I said to her, "Is it hard for you to love your mother? Do you have to learn to love your mother?" And she looked up through her tears, and said, "No; I can't help it; that is spontaneous." "Well," I said, "when the Holy Spirit kindles love in your heart, you cannot help loving God; it will be spontaneous." When the Spirit of God comes into your heart and mine, it will be easy to serve God.

The fruit of the Spirit, as you find it in Galatians, begins with love. There are nine graces spoken of in Galatians 5, and of the nine, Paul puts love at the head of the list; love is the first thing in that precious cluster of fruit. Someone has put it in this way: that all the other eight can be put in the word *love*. Joy is love exulting; peace is love in repose; longsuffering is love on trial; gentleness is love in society; goodness is love in action; faith is love on the battlefield; meekness is love at school; and temperance is love in training. So it is love all the way—love at the top, love at the bottom, and all the way along down these graces.

If we only brought forth the fruit of the Spirit, what a world we would have: There would be no need of any police; a man could leave his overcoat around without someone stealing it; men would not have any desire to do evil. Says Paul, "Against such there is no law"; you don't need any law. A man who is full of the Spirit doesn't need to be put under law; he doesn't need a police officer to watch him. We could dismiss all our police officers; the lawyers would have to give up practicing law; and the courts would not have any business.

THE TRIUMPH OF HOPE

In Romans 15:13 the apostle said: "Now the God of hope fill you with all joy and peace in believing, that you may abound in hope by the power of the Holy Spirit." The next thing, then, is hope.

Did you ever notice this, that no man or woman is ever used by God to build up His kingdom who has lost hope? Now, I have been observing this throughout different parts of the country, and whenever I have found a worker in God's vineyard who has lost hope, I have found a man or woman not very useful. Let your mind go over the past for a moment. Can you think of a man or woman whom God has used to build His kingdom who has lost hope? I don't know of any. It is very important to have hope in the church; and it is the work of the Holy Spirit to impart hope. Let Him come into some of the churches where there has not been any conversions for a few years, and let Him convert a score of people, and see how hopeful the church becomes at once.

He imparts hope; a man filled with the Spirit of God will be very hopeful. He will be looking out into the future and know that it is all bright, because the God of all grace is able to do great things. So it is very important that we have hope.

If a man has lost hope, he is out of communion with God; he has not the Spirit of God resting upon him for service; he may be a son of God, and disheartened so that he cannot be used of God. Do you know there is no place in the Scriptures where it is recorded that God ever used a discouraged man?

Some years ago, I was quite discouraged in my work, and I was ready to hang my harp on the willow. I was very much cast down and depressed. I had been for weeks in that state, when on Monday morning a friend, who had a very large Bible class, came into my study. I used to examine the notes of his Sunday school lessons, which were equal to a sermon, and he came to me this morning and said, "Well, what did you preach about yesterday?" and I told him. I said, "What did you preach about?" and he said that he preached about Noah.

"Did you ever preach about Noah?" he asked me.

"No, I never preached about Noah."

"Did you ever study his character?"

"No, I never studied his life particularly."

"Well," he said, "he is a most wonderful character. It will do you good. You ought to study that character."

When he went out, I took down my Bible and read about Noah; and then it came over me that Noah worked one hundred and twenty years and never had a convert, and yet he did not get discouraged. And I said to myself, *Well, I ought not to be discouraged*, and I closed my Bible, got up, and walked downtown, and the cloud had gone.

I went down to the noon prayer meeting, and heard of a little town in the country where they had taken into the church a hundred young converts; and I thought, *I wonder what Noah would have given if he could have heard that; and yet he worked one hundred and twenty years and didn't get discouraged.* Then a man right across the aisle got up and said: "My friends, I wish you to pray for me; I think I'm lost." Again I said to myself *I wonder what Noah would have given to hear that.* He never heard a man say, "I wish you to pray for me; I think I am lost," and yet he didn't get discouraged!

Oh, children of God, let us not get discouraged. Let us ask God to forgive us, if we have been discouraged and cast down; let us ask God to give us hope, that we may be ever hopeful. It does me good sometimes to meet people and take hold of their hands; they are so hopeful, while other people throw a gloom over me because they are all the time cast down, and looking at the dark side, and looking at the obstacles and difficulties that are in the way.

THE BOON OF LIBERTY

The next thing the Spirit of God does is to give us liberty. He first imparts love; He next inspires hope; and then gives liberty—and that is about the last thing we have in a good many of our churches at the present day. And I am sorry to say there must be a funeral in a good many churches before there is much work done. We shall have to bury the formalism so deep that it will never have any resurrection.

The last thing to be found in many churches is liberty. If the Gospel happens to be preached, the people criticize, as they would a theatrical performance. It is exactly the same, and many a professed Christian never thinks of listening to what the man of God has to say. It is hard work to preach to carnally minded critics, but "where the Spirit of the Lord is, there is liberty" (2 Corinthians 3:17).

A mother may hear a hundred good things in a sermon, and there may be one thing that strikes her as a little out of place, and she will go home and sit down to the table and talk right out before her children and magnify that one wrong thing and not say a word about the hundred good things that were said. That is what men and women do who criticize.

God does not use men in captivity. The condition of many is like Lazarus when he came out of the sepulchre bound hand and foot. The bandage was not taken off his mouth, and he could not speak. He had life, and if you had said Lazarus was not alive, you would have told a falsehood, because he was raised from the dead. There are many people who, the moment you talk to them and insinuate they are not doing what they might, will say: "I have life. I am a Christian." Well, you can't deny it, but they are bound hand and foot.

May God snap these fetters and set His children free, that they may have liberty. I believe He comes to set us free, and wants us to work for Him, and speak for Him. How many people would like to get up in a social prayer meeting to say a few words for Christ, but there is such a cold spirit of criticism in the church that they dare not do it. They have not the liberty to do it. If they get up, they are so frightened with these critics that they begin to tremble and sit down. They cannot say anything. Now, that is all wrong. The Spirit of God comes just to give liberty, and wherever you see the Lord's work going on, you will see that Spirit of liberty. People won't be afraid of speaking to one another. And when the meeting is over they will not get their hats and see how quickly they can get out of the church, but will begin to shake hands with one another, and there will be liberty there.

ALL FROM HIM: LOVE, HOPE, AND LIBERTY

What we need today is love in our hearts. Don't we want it? Don't we want hope in our lives? Don't we want to be hopeful? Don't we want liberty? All this is the work of the Spirit of God, and let us pray God daily to give us love and hope and liberty. We read in Hebrews 10:19, "Having boldness to enter the Holiest by the blood of Jesus." If you will turn to the passage and read the margin, it says: "Having, therefore, brethren, liberty to enter into the Holiest." We can go into the holiest, having freedom of access, and plead for this love and liberty and glorious hope, that we may not rest until God gives us the power to work for Him.

If I know my own heart today, I would rather die than live as I once did, a mere nominal Christian, and not used by God in building up His kingdom. It seems a poor empty life to live for the sake of self.

Let us seek to be useful. Let us seek to be vessels fit for the Master's use, that God, the Holy Spirit, may shine fully through us.

> I am so weak, dear Lord! I can not stand
> One moment without Thee;
> But, oh, the tenderness of Thy enfolding,
> And oh, the faithfulness of Thine upholding,
> And oh, the strength of Thy right hand!
> That strength is enough for me.

I am so needy, Lord! and yet I know
All fullness dwells in Thee;
And hour by hour that never-failing treasure
Supplies and fills in overflowing measure
My last and greatest need. And so
Thy grace is enough for me.

It is so sweet to trust Thy word alone!
I do not ask to see
The unveiling of Thy purpose, or the shining
Of future light on mysteries untwining;
Thy promise-roll is all my own—
Thy word is enough for me.

There were strange soul-depths, restless, vast, and broad,
Unfathomed as the sea,
An infinite craving for some infinite stilling;
But now Thy perfect love is perfect filling!
Lord Jesus Christ, my Lord, my God,
Thou, Thou art enough for me!

—Anon

You remember that strange, half-involuntary "forty years" of Moses in the "wilderness" of Midian, when he had fled from Egypt. You remember, too, the almost equally strange years of retirement in "Arabia" by Paul, when, if ever, humanly speaking, instant action was needed. And pre-eminently you remember the amazing charge of the ascending Lord to the disciples, "Tarry at Jerusalem." Speaking after the manner of men, one could not have wondered if outspoken Peter, or fervid James, had said: "Tarry, Lord! How long?" "Tarry, Lord! is there not a perishing world, groaning for the 'good news?'" "Tarry! Did we hear Thee aright, Lord? Was the word not haste?" Nay; "Being assembled together with them, [He] commanded them that they should not depart from Jerusalem, but wait for the promise of the Father"(Acts 1:4 KJV).

—Grosart

CHAPTER TWO

SECRET POWER: "IN" AND "UPON"

THE HOLY SPIRIT DWELLING IN US is one thing; I think this is clearly brought out in Scripture. The Holy Spirit upon us for service is another thing. Now there are only three places we find in Scripture that are dwelling places for the Holy Spirit.

We find the Spirit dwelling in a special place in Moses' day.

> And he [Moses] raised up the court all around the tabernacle and the altar, and hung up the screen of the court gate. So Moses finished the work. Then the cloud covered the tabernacle of meeting, and the glory of the Lord filled the taberna-

cle. And Moses was not able to enter the tabernacle of meeting, because the cloud rested above it, and the glory of the Lord filled the tabernacle. (Exodus 40:33–35)

GETTING READY

The moment that Moses finished the work, the moment that the tabernacle was ready, the cloud came, the Shekinah glory came and filled it so that Moses was not able to stand before the presence of the Lord. I believe that the moment our hearts are emptied of pride and selfishness and ambition and self-seeking, and everything that is contrary to God's law, the Holy Spirit will come and fill every corner of our hearts. But if we are full of pride and conceit and ambition and self-seeking and pleasure and the world, there is no room for the Spirit of God. I also believe many a man is praying to God to fill him when he is full already with something else. Before we pray that God would fill us, I believe we ought to pray Him to empty us.

There must be an emptying before there can be a filling; and when the heart is turned upside down, and everything is turned out that is contrary to God, then the Spirit will come, just as He did in the tabernacle, and fill us with His glory.

PRAISING IN THE TEMPLE

The second place we find the Spirit of God dwelling is in the temple of Jerusalem. We read in

2 Chronicles 5:13–14:

> Indeed it came to pass, when the trumpeters and
> singers were as one, to make one sound to be heard in
> praising and thanking the Lord, and when they lifted
> up their voice with the trumpets and cymbals and in-
> struments of music, and praised the Lord, saying: "For
> He is good, for His mercy endures forever," that the
> house, the house of the Lord, was filled with a cloud,
> so that the priests could not continue ministering be-
> cause of the cloud; for the glory of the Lord filled the
> house of God.

The very moment that Solomon completed the
temple, when all was finished, they were just praising
God with one heart. The choristers and the singers
and the ministers were all one; there was not any dis-
cord. They were all praising God, and the glory of
God came and just filled the temple, as it had filled the
tabernacle.

POWER ABIDING WITHIN

Now, as you turn over into the New Testament,
you will find, instead of coming to tabernacles and
temples, believers are now the temple of the Holy
Spirit. This is the third resting place of the Spirit.
When, on the day of Pentecost, before Peter preached
that memorable sermon, as they were praying, the
Holy Spirit came and came in mighty power. We now

pray for the Spirit of God to come, and we sing:

> Come, Holy Spirit, heavenly Dove,
> With all Thy quickening power;
> Kindle a flame of heavenly love
> In these cold hearts of ours.

I believe, if we understand it, it is perfectly right; but if we are praying for Him to come out of heaven down to earth again, that is wrong, because He is already here; He has not been out of this earth for more than 1800 years—He has been in the church. He is with all believers; the believers in the church are the called-out ones; they are called out from the world; and every true believer is a temple for the Holy Spirit to dwell in.

In John 14:17 we have the words of Jesus: "The Spirit of truth, whom the world cannot receive, because it neither sees Him nor knows Him; but you know Him, for He dwells with you and will be in you." And now the power of the Holy Spirit is within us, the Scripture says. "Do you not know that you are the temple of God and that the Spirit of God dwells in you?" (1 Corinthians 3:16).

Some time ago, a few men were burying an aged saint. This aged man had been very poor, like many of God's people, poor in this world, but about to be very rich in the other world—about to have all the riches on the other side of life, where thieves cannot get them. They were just hastening him off to the grave, wanting to get rid of him, when an old minister, who was officiating at the grave, said, "Tread softly, for you are carrying the temple of the Holy Spirit." Whenever you see a believer, you see a temple of the Holy Spirit.

In 1 Corinthians 6, Paul reminds believers again of the importance of their bodies as the Spirit's dwelling place: "Do you not know that your body is the temple of the Holy Spirit who is in you, whom you have from God, and you are not your own? For you were bought with a price; therefore glorify God in your body and in your spirit, which are God's" (v. 19–20). Thus are we taught that there is a divine resident in every child of God.

I think it is clearly taught in the Scripture that every believer has the Holy Spirit dwelling in him. He may be quenching the Spirit of God, and he may not glorify God as he should, but if he is a believer on the Lord Jesus Christ, the Holy Spirit dwells in him. But I want to call your attention to another fact: Though Christian men and women have the Holy Spirit dwelling in them, yet He is not dwelling within them in power. In other words, God has a great many sons and daughters without power.

WHAT WE NEED FOR POWER

At least nine-tenths of the church members never think of speaking for Christ. If they see a person, perhaps a near relative, just going right down to ruin, going rapidly, they never think of speaking to him about his sinful course and of seeking to win him to Christ. Now certainly there must be something wrong. And yet when you talk with them, you find they have faith, and you cannot say they are not children of God; but they have not the power, they have not the liberty, they have not the love that real disciples of Christ should have. A great many people are thinking that we need new measures, that we need new churches, that we need new organs, and that we need new choirs, and all these new things. That is not what the church of God needs today. It is the old power that the apostles had; that is what we want, and if we have that in our churches, there will be new life. Then we will have new ministers—the same old ministers renewed with power; filled with the Spirit.

I remember when in Chicago many were toiling in the work, and it seemed as though the car of salvation didn't move on, when a minister began to cry out from the very depths of his heart, "Oh, God, put new ministers in every pulpit." On next Monday I heard two or three men stand up and say, "We had a new minister last Sunday—the same old minister, but he had got new power," and I firmly believe that is what we want today all over America. We want new ministers in the pulpit and new people in the pews. We want people quickened by the Spirit of God, and the Spirit coming down and taking possession of the children of God and giving them power.

Then a man filled with the Spirit will know how to use "the sword of the Spirit." If a man is not filled with the Spirit, he will never know how to use the Book. We are told that this is the sword of the Spirit; and what is an army good for that does not know how to use its weapons? Suppose a battle is going on, and I were a general and had a hundred thousand men, great, able-bodied men, full of life, but not one of them could handle a sword, and not one of them knew how to use his rifle, what would that army be good for? Why, one thousand well-drilled men, with good weapons, would rout the whole of them.

The reason the church cannot overcome the enemy is because she doesn't know how to use the sword of the Spirit. People will get up and try to fight the devil with their experiences, but he doesn't care for that; he will overcome them every time. People are trying to fight the devil with theories and pet ideas, but he will get the victory over them likewise. What we want is to draw the sword of the Spirit. It is that which cuts deeper than anything else.

THE GREATEST WEAPON

Paul gives a great description of our armor for fighting the devil, and he climaxes it with a call to lift up the sword:

> Stand therefore, having girded your waist with truth, having put on the breastplate of righteousness, and

39

having shod your feet with the preparation of the gospel of peace; above all [or over all], taking the shield of faith with which you will be able to quench all the fiery darts of the wicked one. And take the helmet of salvation, and the sword of the Spirit, which is the word of God. (Ephesians 6:14–17)

The sword of the Spirit is the Word of God, and what we need specially is to be filled with the Spirit, so we shall know how to use the Word. There was a Christian man who was using the Word while talking to a skeptic. "I don't believe, sir, in that Book," the skeptic said. The Christian went right on and gave him more of the Word. The skeptic again remarked, "I don't believe the Word"; but the Christian kept giving him more. At last the man was reached; he believed. And the brother added, "When I have proved a good sword that does the work of execution, I would just keep right on using it."

That is what we want. Skeptics and infidels may say they don't believe in it. It is not our work to make them believe in it; that is the work of the Spirit. Our work is to give them the Word of God; not to preach our theories and our ideas about it, but just to deliver the message as God gives it to us. We read in the Scriptures of the sword of the Lord and Gideon. Suppose Gideon had gone out without the sword, he would have been defeated. But the Lord used Gideon; and I think you find all through the Scriptures that

God takes up and uses human instruments. You cannot find, I believe, a case in the Bible where a man is converted without God calling in some human agency—using some human instrument. Not that God cannot do it in His independent sovereignty; there is no doubt about that. Even when by the revealed glory of the Lord Jesus, Saul of Tarsus was smitten to the earth, Ananias was used to open his eyes and lead him into the light of the Gospel. I heard a man once say, if you put a man on a mountain peak, higher than one of the Alpine peaks, God could save him without a human messenger; but that is not His way; that is not His method; but it is "the sword of the Lord and Gideon." The Lord and Gideon will do the work; and if we are just willing to let the Lord use us, He will.

NONE OF SELF

Then you will find all through the Scriptures, when men were filled with the Holy Spirit, they preached Christ and not themselves. They preached Christ and Him crucified. So the father of John the Baptist could prophesy. "Now his father Zacharias was filled with the Holy Spirit, and prophesied, saying: 'Blessed is the Lord God of Israel, for He has visited and redeemed His people, and has raised up a horn of salvation for us in the house of His servant David, as He spoke by the mouth of His holy prophets'" (Luke 1:67–70).

See, Zacharias was talking about the Word. If a man is filled with the Spirit, he will magnify the Word;

41

he will preach the Word, and not himself; he will give this lost world the Word of the living God. Here are more words from Zacharias under the Spirit's power: "And you, child, will be called the prophet of the Highest; for you will go before the face of the Lord to prepare His ways, to give knowledge of salvation to His people by the remission of their sins, through the tender mercy of our God, with which the Dayspring from on high has visited us; to give light to those who sit in darkness and the shadow of death, to guide our feet into the way of peace" (Luke 1:76–79).

We also find that Simeon, as he came into the temple and found the young child Jesus there, at once began to quote the Scriptures, for the Spirit was upon him. And when Peter stood up on the day of Pentecost, and preached that wonderful sermon, it is said he was filled with the Holy Spirit, and began to preach the Word to the multitude, and it was the Word that cut them. It was the sword of the Lord and Peter, the same as it was the sword of the Lord and Gideon. And we find it says of Stephen, "They were not able to resist the wisdom and the Spirit by which he spoke" (Acts 6:10). Why? Because he gave them the Word of God. And we are told that the Holy Spirit came on Stephen, and none could resist his words.

We read, too, that Paul was full of the Holy Spirit, and that he preached Christ and Him crucified, and that many people were added to the church. Barnabas was full of faith and the Holy Spirit; and if you will just read and find out what he preached, you will find it was the Word, and many were added to the Lord. So that when a man is full of the Spirit, he begins to preach, not himself, but Christ, as revealed in the Holy Scriptures.

The disciples of Jesus were all filled with the Spirit, and the Word was published; and when the Spirit of God comes down upon the church, and we are anointed, the Word will be published in the streets, in the lanes, and in the alleys. There will not be a dark cellar nor a dark attic, nor a home where the Gospel will not be carried by some loving heart, if the Spirit comes upon God's people in demonstration and in power.

SPIRITUAL IRRIGATION

It is possible a man may just barely have life and be satisfied, and I think that a great many are in that condition. In John 3 we find that Nicodemus came to Christ and that he received life. At first this life was feeble. You don't hear of him standing up confessing Christ boldly and of the Spirit coming upon him in great power, though he possessed life through faith in Christ. And then turn to John 4, and you will find it speaks of the woman coming to the well of Samaria; Christ held out the cup of salvation to her and she took it and drank, and it became in her "a fountain of water springing up into everlasting life" (v. 14). That is better than in John 3; here it came down in a flood into her soul. As someone has said, it came down from the throne of God, and like a mighty current carried her back to the throne of God. Water always rises to its level, and if we get the soul filled with water from the throne of God, it will bear us upward to its source.

But if you want to get the best class of Christian life portrayed, turn to the seventh chapter and you will find that it says he who receives the Spirit, through trusting in the Lord Jesus, "out of his heart will flow rivers of living water" (v. 38). Now there are two ways of digging a well. As a boy upon a farm in New England with a well, I used to have to pump the water from an old wooden pump on wash day and water the cattle. I had to pump and pump and pump until my arm got tired, many a time. But they have a better way now; they don't dig down a few feet and brick up the hole and put the pump in, but they go down through the clay and the sand and the rock, and on down until they strike what they call a lower stream. Then it becomes an artesian well, which needs no labor, as the water rises spontaneously from the depths beneath.

Now I think God wants all His children to be a sort of artesian well; not to keep pumping, but to flow right out. Why, haven't you seen ministers in the pulpit just pumping and pumping and pumping? I have, many a time, and I have had to do it, too. I know how it is. They stand in the pulpit and talk and talk and talk, and the people go to sleep; they can't arouse them. What is the trouble? Why, the living water is not there; they are just pumping when there is no water in the well. You can't get water out of a dry well; you have to get something in the well, or you can't get anything out. I have seen these wooden pumps where you had to pour water into them before you could pump any water out, and so it is with a good many people; you have to get something in them before you can get anything out.

People wonder why it is that they have no spiritual power. They stand up and talk in meeting, and don't say anything; they say they haven't anything to say, and you find it out soon enough; they need not state it; but they just talk, because they feel it is a duty, and say nothing.

Now I tell you, when the Spirit of God is resting upon us for service, we are anointed, and then we can do great things. "I will pour water on him that is thirsty," says God. Oh, blessed thought: "Those who hunger and thirst for righteousness . . . shall be filled" (Matthew 5:6).

OUTFLOWING STREAMS

I would like to see people full of living water—so full that they couldn't contain it; that they would have to go out and publish the gospel of the grace of God. When a man gets so full he can't hold any more, then he is just ready for God's service.

When preaching in Chicago, Dr. Gibson remarked in the inquiry meeting, "Now, how can we find out who is thirsty?" Then he said, "I was just thinking how we could find out. If a boy should come down the aisle, bringing a good pail of clear water and a dipper, we would soon find out who was thirsty; we would see thirsty men and women reach out for water; but if you should walk down the aisle with an empty bucket, you wouldn't find it out. People would look in and see that there was no water, and say nothing.

"I think that is the reason we are not more blessed in our ministry. We are carrying around empty buckets, and the people see that we have not anything in them, and they don't come forward."

I think that there is a good deal of truth in that. People see that we are carrying around empty buckets, and they will not come to us until they are filled. They see we haven't any more than they have. We must have the Spirit of God resting upon us, and then we will have something that gives the victory over the world, the flesh, and the devil; something that gives the victory over our tempers, over our conceits, and over every other evil. When we can trample these sins under our feet, then people will come to us and say, "How did you get it? I need this power. You have something that I haven't got; I want it."

Oh, may God show us this truth. Have we been toiling all night? Let us throw the net on the right side; let us ask God to forgive our sins, and anoint us with power from on high. But remember, He is not going to give this power to an impatient man; He is not going to give it to a selfish man; He will never give it to an ambitious man whose aim is selfish. One must first be emptied of self, emptied of pride, and emptied of all worldly thoughts.

Let it be God's glory and not our own that we seek, and when we get to that point, how speedily the Lord will bless us for good.

Then will the measure of our blessing be full. Do you know what heaven's measure is? "Good measure, pressed down, shaken together, and running over" (Luke 6:38). If we get our hearts filled with the Word of God, how is Satan going to get in? How is the world going to get in, for heaven's measure is good measure, full measure, running over.

Have you this fullness? If you have not, then seek it; say by the grace of God you will have it, for it is the Father's good pleasure to give us these things. He wants us to shine in this world; He wants to lift us up for His work; He wants us to have the power to testify for His Son. He has left us in this world to testify for Him. What did He leave us for? Not to buy and sell and to get gain, but to glorify Christ. How are you going to do it without the Spirit? That is the question. How are you going to do it without the power of God?

WHY SOME FAIL

We read in John 20:22: "And when He had said this, He breathed on them, and said to them, 'Receive the Holy Spirit.'" Then see Luke 24:49: "Behold, I send the Promise of My Father upon you; but tarry in the city of Jerusalem until you are endued with power from on high."

The first passage tells us He had raised those pierced and wounded hands over them and breathed upon them and said, "Receive the Holy Spirit." And I haven't a doubt they received it then, but not in such mighty power as afterward when qualified for their work. It was not in fullness that He gave it to them then, but if they had been like a good many now, they would have said, "I have enough now; I am not going to tarry; I am going to work."

Some people seem to think they are losing time if they wait on God for His power, and so away they go and work without unction; they are working without any anointing, without any power. But after Jesus had said "Receive the Holy Spirit," and had breathed on them, He said: "Now you tarry in Jerusalem until you be endued with power from on high." Read in Acts 1:8, "But you shall receive power when the Holy Spirit has come upon you."

Now, the Spirit had been given them certainly or they could not have believed, and they could not have taken their stand for God and gone through what they did, and endured the scoffs and frowns of their friends, if they had not been converted by the power of the Holy Spirit. But now just see what Christ said:

"You shall receive power when the Holy Spirit has come upon you; and you shall be witnesses to Me in Jerusalem, and in all Judea and Samaria, and to the end of the earth" (Acts 1:8).

Then, the Holy Spirit *in* us is one thing, and the Holy Spirit *on* us is another; and if these Christians had gone out and went right to preaching then and there, without the power, do you think that scene would have taken place on the day of Pentecost? Don't you think that Peter would have stood up there and beat against the air, while these Jews would have gnashed their teeth and mocked him? But they tarried in Jerusalem; they waited ten days. "What!" you say. "What, the world perishing and men dying! Shall I wait?" Do what God tells you. There is no use in running before you are sent; there is no use in attempting to do God's work without God's power. A man working without this unction, a man working without this anointing, a man working without the Holy Spirit upon him, is losing his time after all. So we are not going to lose anything if we tarry till we get this power. That is the object of true service, to wait on God, to tarry until we receive this power for witness-bearing.

Then we find that on the day of Pentecost, ten days after Jesus Christ was glorified, the Holy Spirit descended in power. Do you think that Peter and James and John and those apostles doubted it from that very hour? They never doubted it. Perhaps some question the possibility of having the power of God now, and that the Holy Spirit never came afterward in similar manifestation, and will never come again in such power.

FRESH SUPPLIES

Turn to Acts 4:31, and you will find He came a second time, and at a place where they were, so that the earth was shaken, and they were filled with this power. The fact is, we are leaky vessels, and we have to keep right under the fountain all the time to keep full of Christ, and so have a fresh supply.

I believe this is a mistake a great many of us are making; we are trying to do God's work with the grace God gave us ten years ago. We say, if it is necessary, we will go on with the same grace. Now, what we want is a fresh supply, a fresh anointing and fresh power, and if we seek it, and seek it with all our hearts, we will obtain it.

The early converts were taught to look for that power. Philip went to Samaria, and news reached Jerusalem that there was a great work being done in Samaria, and many converts. So John and Peter went down, and they laid their hands on them, and they received the Holy Spirit for service. I think that is what we Christians ought to be looking for—the Spirit of God for service—that God may use us mightily in the building up of His church and hastening His glory.

In Acts 19 we read of twelve men at Ephesus, who, when the inquiry was made if they had received the Holy Spirit since they believed, answered: "We have not so much as heard whether there is a Holy Spirit" (v. 2). I venture to say there are very many, who, if you were to ask them, "Have you received the Holy Spirit since you believed?" would reply, "I don't know what you mean by that." They would be like the twelve men down at Ephesus, who had never understood the peculiar relation of the Spirit to the sons of God in this dispensation. I firmly believe that the church has just laid this knowledge aside, mislaid it somewhere, and so Christians are without power. Sometimes you can take one hundred members into the church, and they don't add to its power. Now that is all wrong. If they were only anointed by the Spirit of God, there would be great power if one hundred saved ones were added to the church.

GREEN FIELDS

When I was out in California, the first time I went down from the Sierra Nevada Mountains and dropped into the valley of the Sacramento, I was surprised to find on one farm that everything about it was green— all the trees and flowers, everything was blooming, and everything was green and beautiful. Just across the hedge everything was dried up, and there was not a green thing there, and I could not understand it. I made inquiries, and I found that the man on the beautiful farm had turned everything green by irrigating it. He just poured the water right on, and he kept everything green, while the fields that were next to his were as dry as Gideon's fleece without a drop of dew.

Many in the church today are like those farms in

California—they're dreary deserts, everything parched and desolate, and apparently no life in them. They can sit next to a man who is full of the Spirit of God, who is like a green bay tree, and who is bringing forth fruit, and yet they will not seek a similar blessing. Well, why this difference? Because God has poured water on him that was thirsty; that is the difference. One has been seeking this anointing, and he has received it; and when we want this above everything else, God will surely give it to us.

The great question before us now is *do* we want it? I remember when I first went to England and gave a Bible reading—I think about the first that I gave in that country—a great many ministers were there, and I didn't know anything about English theology. I was afraid I should run against their creeds, and I was a little hampered, especially on this very subject, about the gift of the Holy Spirit for service. I remember particularly a Christian minister there who had his head bowed on his hand, and I thought the good man was ashamed of everything I was saying, and of course that troubled me. At the close of my address he took his hat and went away, and then I thought, "Well, I shall never see him again."

At the next meeting I looked all around for him and he wasn't there, and at the next meeting I looked again, but he was absent; and I thought my teaching must have given him offense. But a few days after that, at a large noon prayer meeting, a man stood up and his face shone as if he had been up in the mountain with God, and I looked at him, and to my great joy it was this brother. He said he was at that Bible reading, and he heard there was such a thing as having fresh power to preach the Gospel; he made up his mind that if that was for him he would have it. He said he went home and looked to the Master, and that he never had such a battle with himself in his life. He asked that God would show him the sinfulness of his heart that he knew nothing about, and he just cried mightily to God that he might be emptied of himself and filled with the Spirit; and he said, "God has answered my prayer."

I met him in Edinburgh six months from that date, and he told me he had preached the Gospel every night during that time, that he had not preached one sermon but that some remained for conversation, and that he had engagements four months ahead to preach the Gospel every night in different churches. I think you could have fired a cannonball right through his church and not hit anyone before he got this anointing; but it was not thirty days before the building was full and aisles crowded. He had his bucket filled full of fresh water, and the people found it out and came flocking to him from every quarter. I tell you, you can't get the stream higher than the fountain. What we need very specially is power.

There was another man whom I have in my mind, and he said, "I have heart disease, I can't preach more than once a week," so he had a colleague to preach for him and do the visiting. He was an old minister, and couldn't do any visiting. He had heard of this anointing, and he said, "I would like to be anointed for my burial. I would like before I go hence to have just one more privilege to preach the Gospel with power." He prayed that God would fill him with the Spirit, and I met him not long after that, and he said, "I have preached on an average eight times a week, and I have had conversions all along." The Spirit came on him. I don't believe that man broke down at first with hard work as much as with using the machinery without oil, without lubrication. It is not the hard work that breaks down ministers, but it is the toil of working without power.

Oh, that God may anoint his people! Not the ministry alone, but every disciple. Do not suppose pastors are the only laborers needing it. There is not a mother but needs it in her house to regulate her family, just as much as the minister needs it in the pulpit or the Sunday school teacher needs it in his class. We all need it together, and let us not rest day or night until we possess it. If that is the uppermost thought in our hearts, God will give it to us if we just hunger and thirst for it, and say, "God helping me, I will not rest until endued with power from on high."

MASTER AND SERVANT

The time had come for Elijah to be taken up, and he said to Elisha, "You stay here at Gilgal, and I will go up to Bethel." There was a theological seminary there, and some young students, and he wanted to see how they were getting along; but Elisha said, "As the Lord lives, and as your soul lives, I will not leave you!" So Elisha just kept close to Elijah. They came to Bethel, and the sons of the prophets came out and said to Elisha, "'Do you know that the Lord will take your master from over you today?' And Elisha said, 'Yes, I know; but keep silent!' Then Elijah said to him, 'Stay here at Bethel, for the Lord has sent me on to Jericho.' But Elisha said, 'As the Lord lives and your soul lives, I will not leave you!'" (See 2 Kings 2:2–4.)

"You shall not go without me," said Elisha; and then I can imagine that Elisha just put his arm in that of Elijah, and they walked down together. I can see those two mighty men walking down to Jericho, and when they arrived there, the sons of the prophets came and said to Elisha, "Do you know that your master is to be taken away?"

"Hush! keep still," says Elisha, "I know it."

And then Elijah said to Elisha, "Stay here awhile, for the Lord has sent me on to Jericho." But Elisha said, "I will not leave you."

And then Elisha came right close to Elijah; and when they came to the Jordan, Elijah took off his mantle and struck the waters, and they "divided this way and that, so that the two of them crossed over" like giants, dry-shod, and fifty sons of the prophets came to look at them and watch them (see vv. 7–8). They didn't know, but Elijah would be taken up right in their sight. As they passed over Jordan, Elijah said to Elisha, "Now, what do you want?" He knew he was after something. "What can I do for you? Just make your request known."

"I would like a double portion of your Spirit."

I can imagine now that Elijah had given him a chance to ask; he said to himself, "I will ask for enough." Elisha had a good deal of the Spirit, but he said, "I want a double portion of thy Spirit." "Well," says Elijah, "if you see me when I am taken up, you shall have it."

Do you think you could have enticed Elisha from Elijah at that moment? I can almost see the two, arm in arm, walking along, and as they walked, there came along the chariot of fire, and before Elisha knew it, Elijah was caught up, and as he went sweeping toward the throne, the servant cried, "My Father! My Father! The chariot of Israel and its horsemen!" (v. 12).

Elisha saw him no more. He picked up Elijah's fallen mantle, and returning with that old mantle of his masters, he came to the Jordan and cried for Elijah's God, and the waters separated, and he passed through dry-shod. Then the watching prophets lifted up their voices and said, "The Spirit of Elijah rests upon Elisha" and so it was, a double portion of it.

May the Spirit of Elijah, beloved reader, be upon us. If we seek for it, we shall find it. Oh, may the God of Elijah answer by fire, and consume the spirit of worldliness in the churches, burn up the dross, and make us wholehearted Christians! May that Spirit come upon us; let that be our prayer in our family altars and in our closets!

Let us cry mightily to God that we may have a double portion of the Holy Spirit, and that we may not rest satisfied with this worldly state of living; let us, like Samson, shake ourselves and come out from the world, that we may have the power of God!

A man may as well hew marble without tools, or paint without colors or instruments, or build without materials, as perform any acceptable service without the graces of the Spirit, which are both the materials and the instruments in the work.

—Alleine

*I*f we do not have the Spirit of God, it were better to shut the churches, to nail up the doors, to put a black cross on them, and say, "God have mercy on us!" If you ministers have not the Spirit of God, you had better not preach, and you people had better stay at home. I think I speak not too strongly when I say that a church in the land without the Spirit of God is rather a curse than a blessing. If you have not the Spirit of God, Christian worker, remember that you stand in somebody else's way; you are as a tree bearing no fruit standing where another fruitful tree might grow. This is solemn work; the Holy Spirit or nothing, and worse than nothing.

—Spurgeon

CHAPTER THREE
WITNESSING IN POWER

THE SUBJECT OF WITNESSING in the power of the Holy Spirit is not sufficiently understood by the church. Until we have more intelligence on this point, we are laboring under great disadvantage.

In John 15:26–27, you will find these words: "But when the Helper comes, whom I will send to you from the Father, the Spirit of truth who proceeds from the Father, He will testify of Me. And you also will bear witness, because you have been with Me from the beginning." Here we find what the Spirit is going to do, or what Christ said He would do when He came; namely, that He should testify of Him. And in Acts 2, you will find that when Peter stood up on the day of Pentecost, and testified of what Christ had done, the Holy Spirit came down and bore witness to that fact, and men were convicted by hundreds and by thousands. So then man cannot preach effectively of himself. He must have the Spirit of God to give ability, and study God's Word in order to testify according to the mind of the Spirit.

WHAT IS THE TESTIMONY?

If we keep back the gospel of Christ and do not bring Christ before the people, then the Spirit has not the opportunity to work. But the moment Peter stood up on the day of Pentecost and bore testimony to this one fact, that Christ died for sin, and that He had been raised again and ascended into heaven—the Spirit came down to bear witness to the person and work of Christ.

If it were not for the Holy Spirit bearing witness to the preaching of the facts of the Gospel, do you think that the church would have lived during these last eighteen centuries? Do you believe that Christ's death, resurrection, and ascension would not have been forgotten as soon as His birth, if it had not been for the fact that the Holy Spirit had come? Because it is very clear, that when John made his appearance on the borders of the wilderness, they had forgotten all about the birth of Jesus Christ. Just thirty short years. It was all gone.

They had forgotten the story of the shepherds; they had forgotten the wonderful scene that took place in the temple, when the Son of God was brought and the older prophets and prophetesses were there. They had forgotten about the wise men coming to Jerusalem to inquire where He was that was born King of the Jews. That story of His birth seemed to have just faded away. They had forgotten all about it, and when John made his appearance on the borders of the wilderness it was brought back to their minds. And if it had not been for the Holy Spirit coming down to bear witness to Christ, to testify of His death and resurrection, those facts would have been forgotten as soon as His birth.

GREATER WORK

The witness of the Spirit is the witness of power. Jesus said, "The works that I do he will do also; and greater works than these he will do, because I go to My Father" (John 14:12). I used to stumble over that. I didn't understand it. I thought, what greater work could any man do than Christ had done? How could anyone raise a dead man who had been laid away in the sepulchre for days, and who had already begun to turn back to dust; how with a word could He call him forth? But the longer I live, the more I am convinced it is a greater thing to influence a man's will—a man whose will is set against God—to have that will broken and brought into subjection to God's will. In other words, it is a greater thing to have power over a living, sinning, God-hating man than to raise the dead.

He who could create a world could speak a dead soul into life; but I think the greatest miracle this world has seen was the miracle at Pentecost. Here were men who surrounded the apostles, full of prejudice, full of malice, full of bitterness, their hands, as it were, dripping with the blood of the Son of God. Yet an unlettered man—a man whom they hated—stood up and preached the Gospel, and three thousand of them were immediately convicted and converted. They became disciples of the Lord Jesus Christ and were willing to lay down their lives for the Son of God. It may have been on that occasion that Stephen was converted, the first martyr, and some of the men who soon after would give up their lives for Christ. This seems to me the greatest miracle this world has ever seen. But Peter did not labor alone; the Spirit of God was with him; hence the marvelous results.

The Jewish law required that there should be two witnesses, and so we find that when Peter preached there was a second witness. Peter testified of Christ, and Christ said that when the Holy Spirit would come, "He will testify of me." And they both bore witness to the verities of our Lord's incarnation, ministry, death, and resurrection, and the result was that a multitude turned as with one heart unto the Lord.

Our failure now is that preachers ignore the Cross, and veil Christ with sapless sermons and superfine language. They don't just present Him to the people plainly, and that is why I believe that the Spirit of God doesn't work with power in our churches. What we need is, to preach Christ and present Him to a perishing world. The world can get on very well without you and me, but the world cannot get on without Christ, and therefore we must testify of Him.

The world today is hungering and thirsting for this divine, satisfying portion. Thousands and thousands are sitting in darkness, knowing not of this great Light, but when we begin to preach Christ honestly, faithfully, sincerely, and truthfully—holding Him up, not ourselves; exalting Christ and not our theories; presenting Christ and not our opinions; advocating Christ and not some false doctrine—then the Holy Spirit will come and bear witness. He will testify that what we say is true. When He comes, He will confirm the Word with signs following.

This is one of the strongest proofs that our Gospel is divine; that it is of divine origin: Not only did Christ teach these things, but when leaving the world He said, "He will glorify me," and "He will testify of me." Just look at Acts 2:36, and you will read these words: "Therefore let all the house of Israel know assuredly that God has made this Jesus, whom you crucified, both Lord and Christ." And when Peter said this, the Holy Spirit descended upon the people and testified of Christ—bore witness in signal demonstration that all this was true. And again, in verse 40, "And with many other words he testified and exhorted them, saying, 'Be saved from this perverse generation.'" With many other words did He testify; not only these words that have been recorded, but many other words.

THE SURE GUIDE

Turn to John 16:13, and read: "However, when He, the Spirit of truth, has come, He will guide you into all truth; for He will not speak on His own authority; but whatever He hears He will speak; and He will tell you things to come." He will guide you into all truth. Now there is not a truth that we ought to know but the Spirit of God will guide us into it if we will let Him. If we will yield ourselves to be directed by the Spirit, and let Him lead us, He will guide us into all truth. It would have saved us from a great many dark hours if we had only been willing to let the Spirit of God be our counselor and guide.

Lot never would have gone to Sodom if he had been guided by the Spirit of God. David never would have fallen into sin and had all that trouble with his family, if he had been guided by the Spirit of God.

There are many Lots and Davids today. The churches are full of them. Men and women are in total darkness, because they have not been willing to be guided by the Spirit of God. "He will guide you into all truth: for he shall not speak of himself" (John 16:13 KJV). He shall speak of the ascended, glorified Christ.

What would be thought of a messenger, entrusted by an absent husband with a message for his wife or mother, who, on arrival, only talked of himself and his conceits, and ignored both the husband and the message? You would simply call it outrageous. What then must be the crime of the professed teacher who speaks of himself, or some insipid theory, leaving out Christ and His Gospel? If we witness according to the Spirit, we must witness of Jesus.

The Holy Spirit is down here in this dark world to just speak of the Absent One, and He takes the things of Christ and brings them to our mind. He testifies of Christ; He guides us into the truth about Him.

RAPPINGS IN THE DARK

Many children of God today are turning aside and committing a grievous sin. I don't know as they think it is a sin, but if we examine the Scriptures, we will find that it is a great sin. We are told that the Helper is sent into the world to "guide [us] into all truth," and if He is sent for that purpose, do we need any other guide? Need we hide in the darkness, consulting with mediums, who profess to call up the spirits of the dead? Do you know what the Word of God pronounces against that fearful sin? I believe it is one of the greatest sins we have to contend with at the present day. It is dishonoring to the Holy Spirit for me to go and summon up the dead and confer with them, even if it were possible.

Notice 1 Chronicles 10:13–14: "So Saul died for his unfaithfulness which he had committed against the Lord, because he did not keep the word of the Lord, and also because he consulted a medium for guidance. But he did not inquire of the Lord; therefore He killed him, and turned the kingdom over to David the son of Jesse."

God killed him for this very sin. Of the two sins that are brought against Saul here, one is that he would not keep the Word of God, and the second is that he consulted a familiar spirit. He was snared by this great evil and sinned against God.

Saul fell right here, and there are a great many of God's professed children today who think there is no harm in consulting a medium who pretends to call up some of the departed to inquire of them.

But how dishonoring it is to God who has sent the Holy Spirit into this world to guide us "into all truth." There is not one thing that I need to know, there is not a thing that is important for me to know; there is not a thing that I ought to know but the Spirit of God will reveal it to me through the Word of God, and if I turn my back upon the Holy Spirit, I am dishonoring the Spirit of God, and I am committing a grievous sin.

We read in Luke, where that rich man in the other world wanted to have someone sent to his father's house to warn his five brothers. Christ said: "If they do not hear Moses and the prophets, neither will they be persuaded though one rise from the dead" (Luke 16:31). Moses and the prophets, the part of the Bible then completed, that is enough. But a great many people now want something besides the Word of God, and are turning aside to these false lights.

There is another passage which reads, "And when they say to you, 'Seek those who are mediums and wizards, who whisper and mutter,' should not a people seek their God?" (Isaiah 8:19). What is that but table-rapping, and cabinet-hiding? If it were a message from God, do you think you would have to go into a dark room and put out all the lights? In secret my Master taught nothing. God is not in that movement, and what we want as children of God is to keep ourselves from this evil.

NO LIGHT IN THEM

And then notice the verse following, quoted so often out of its connection. "To the law and to the testimony! If they do not speak according to this word, it is because there is no light in them." Any man and any woman who comes to us with any doctrine that is not according to the law and the testimony, let us understand that they are from the evil one, and that they are enemies of righteousness. They have no light in them. Now you will find that these people who are consulting familiar spirits, first and last attack the Word of God. They don't believe it. Still a great many people say, you must hear both sides. But if a man should write me a most slanderous letter about my wife, I don't think I would have to read it; I should tear it up and throw it to the winds. Have I to read all the infidel books that are written, to hear both sides? Have I to take up a book that is a slander on my Lord and Master, who has redeemed me with His blood? Ten thousand times "no"; I will not touch it.

"Now the Spirit expressly says that in latter times some will depart from the faith, giving heed to deceiving spirits and doctrines of demons" (1 Timothy 4:1). That is pretty plain language, isn't it? "Doctrines of demons." Again, "speaking lies in hypocrisy, having their own conscience seared with a hot iron" (4:2). There are other passages of Scripture warning against every delusion of Satan. Let us ever remember the Spirit has been sent into the world to guide us into all truth. We don't want any other guide; He is enough.

Some people say, "Is not conscience a safer guide than the Word and the Spirit?" No, it is not. Some people don't seem to have any conscience, and don't know what it means. Their education has a good deal to do with conscience. There are persons who will say that their conscience did not tell them that they had done wrong until after the wrong was done; but what we want is something to tell us a thing is wrong before we do it. Very often a man will go and commit some awful crime, and after it is done his conscience will wake up and lash and scourge him, and then it is too late—the act is done.

THE UNERRING GUIDE

I am told by people who have been over the Alps, that the guide fastens them, if they are going in a dangerous place, right to himself, and he just goes on before; they are fastened to the guide.

And so should the Christian be linked to His unerring Guide, and be safely upheld. Why, if a man was going through the Mammoth Cave, it would be death to him if he strayed away from his guide. If separated from him, he would certainly perish; there are pitfalls in that cave and a bottomless river, and there would be no chance for a man to find his way through that cave without a guide or a light. So there is no chance for us to get through the dark wilderness of this world alone. It is folly for a man or woman to think one can get through this evil world without the light of God's Word and the guidance of the divine Spirit. God sent Him to guide us through this great journey, and if we seek to work independent of Him, we shall stumble into the deep darkness of eternity's night.

But bear in mind the *words* of the Spirit of God; if you want to be guided, you must study the Word, because the Word is the light of the Spirit. In John 14:26, we read: "But the Helper, the Holy Sprit, whom the Father will send in My name, He will teach you all things, and bring to your remembrance all things that I said to you." Again, in John 16:13: "However, when He, the Spirit of truth, has come, He will guide you into all truth; for He will not speak on His own authority, but whatever He hears, He will speak; and He will tell you things to come."

"He will tell you things to come." A great many

people seem to think that the Bible is out of date, that it is an old book, and they think it has passed its day. They say it was very good for the Dark Ages, and that there is some very good history in it; but then it was not intended for the present time; that we are living in a very enlightened age, and that men can get on very well without the old Book; we have outgrown it. They think we have no use for it, because it is an old book. Now you might just as well say that the sun, which has shone so long, is now so old that it is out of date, and that whenever a man builds a house he need not put any windows in it, because we have got a newer light and a better light; we have gaslight and this new electric light. These are something new; and I would advise people, if they think the Bible is too old and worn out, when they build their houses, not to put any windows in them, but just to light them with this new electric light; that is something new, and this is what they are anxious for.

People talk about this Book as if they understood it; but we don't know much about it yet. The press gives us the daily news of what has taken place. This Bible, however, tells us what is about to take place. This *is* new; we have the news here in this Book; this tells us of the things that will surely come to pass; and that is a great deal newer than anything in the newspapers.

The Bible tells us that the Spirit shall teach us all things; not only guide us into all truth, but teach us all things. He teaches us how to pray, and I don't think there has ever been a prayer upon this sin-cursed earth that has been indicted by the Holy Spirit but was answered. There is much praying that is not indicted by the Holy Spirit. In former years I was very ambitious to get rich. I used to pray for one hundred thousand dollars; that was my aim, and I used to say, "God does not answer my prayer; He does not make me rich." But I had no warrant for such a prayer; yet a good many people pray in that way; they think that they pray, but they do not pray according to the Scriptures. The Spirit of God has nothing to do with their prayers, and such prayers are not the product of His teaching.

It is the Spirit that teaches us how to answer our enemies. If a man strikes me, I should not pull out a revolver and shoot him. The Spirit of the Lord doesn't teach me revenge; He doesn't teach me that it is necessary to draw the sword and cut a man down in order to defend my rights. Some people say, "You are a coward if you don't strike back." Christ says, "Turn the other cheek to him who smites." I would rather take Christ's teaching than any other. I don't think a man gains much by loading himself down with weapons to defend himself. There has been life enough sacrificed in this country to teach men a lesson in this regard. The Word of God is a much better protection than the revolver. We had better take the Word of God to protect us, by accepting its teaching and living out its precepts.

AN AID TO MEMORY

It is a great comfort to us to remember that another office of the Spirit is to bring the teaching of Jesus to our remembrance. This was our Lord's promise, "He will teach you all things, and bring to your remembrance all things" (John 14: 26).

How striking that is! I think there are many Christians who have had that experience. They have been testifying, and found that the Spirit, while talking for Christ, has just brought into mind some of the sayings of the Lord Jesus Christ, and their mind was soon filled with the Word of God. When we have the Spirit resting upon us, we can speak with authority and power, and the Lord will bless our testimony and bless our work. I believe the reason why God makes use of so few in the church is because there is not in them the power that God can use. He is not going to use our ideas, but we must have the Word of God hid in our hearts. Then, the Holy Spirit inflaming us, we will have the testimony that will be rich, and sweet, and fresh, and the Lord's Word will vindicate itself in blessed results.

God wants to use us; God wants to make us channels of blessing; but we are in such a condition He does not use us. That is the trouble; there are so many believers who have no testimony for the Lord; if they speak, they speak without saying anything, and if they pray, their prayer is powerless. They do not plead in prayer; their prayer is just a few set phrases that you have heard too often. Now, what we want is to be so full of the Word that the Spirit coming upon us shall bring to mind—bring to our remembrance—the words of the Lord Jesus.

In 1 Corinthians 2:9, it is written: "Eye has not seen, nor ear heard, nor have entered into the heart of man the things which God has prepared for those who love Him."

We hear that quoted so often in prayer—many Christians weave it into their prayers and stop right there. And the moment you talk about heaven, they say, "Oh, we don't know anything about heaven; eye has not seen; it is all speculation. We have nothing to do with it; and they say they quote it as it is written." But look at what's next, in verse 10: "But God has revealed them to us through His Spirit." The Lord *does* reveal them to us. How? "For the Spirit searches all things, yes, the deep things of God." That is just what the Spirit does.

LONG AND SHORT SIGHT

He brings to our mind what God has in store for us. I heard a man, some time ago, speaking about Abraham. He said: "Abraham was not tempted by the well-watered plains of Sodom, for Abraham was what you might call a longsighted man; he had his eyes set on the city which had foundation—'whose Builder and Maker is God.'" But Lot was a shortsighted man; and there are many people in the church who are very shortsighted; they only see things right around them they think good. Abraham was longsighted; he had glimpses of the celestial city. Moses was longsighted, and he left the palaces of Egypt and identified himself with God's people—poor people, who were slaves; but he had something in view yonder; he could see something God had in store.

Some people are sort of longsighted and short-sighted, too. I have a friend who has one eye that is longsighted and the other is shortsighted; and I think the church is full of this kind of people. They want one eye for the world and the other for the kingdom of God. Therefore, everything is blurred: One eye is long and the other is short, all is confusion. The church is filled with that sort of people.

But Stephen was longsighted; he looked clear into heaven; they couldn't convince him, even when he was dying, that Christ had not ascended to heaven. "Look, look yonder," he says, "I see Him over there; He is on the throne, standing at the right hand of God"; and he looked clear into heaven (see Acts 7:55–56). The world had no temptation for him; he had put the world under his feet. Paul was another of those longsighted men; he had been caught up and seen things unlawful for him to utter; things grand and glorious. I tell you when the Spirit of God is on us, the world looks very empty; the world has a very small hold upon us, and we begin to let go of our hold on it.

When the Spirit of God is on us, we will just let go the things of time and lay hold of things eternal. This is the church's need today; we want the Spirit to come in mighty power, and consume all the vile dross there is in us. Oh, that the Spirit of fire may come down and burn everything in us that is contrary to God's blessed Word and will!

In John 14:16 (KJV), we read of the Comforter. This is the first time He is spoken of as the Comforter. Christ had been their Comforter. God had sent Him to comfort the sorrowing. It was prophesied of Him, "The Spirit of the Lord is upon Me, because He has anointed Me to preach the gospel to the poor; He has sent me to heal the brokenhearted" (Luke 4:18). You can't heal the brokenhearted without the Comforter; but the world would not have the first Comforter, and so they rose up and took Him to Calvary and put him to death; but on going away He said, "I will send you another Comforter; you shall not be comfortless; be of good cheer, little flock; it is the Father's good pleasure to give you the kingdom" (see John 14:16; Luke 12:32). All these sweet passages are brought to the remembrance of God's people, and they help us to rise out of the fog and mist of this world. Oh, what a comforter is the Holy Spirit of God!

THE FAITHFUL FRIEND

The Holy Spirit tells a man of his faults in order to lead him to a better life. In John 16:8, we read, "He will convict the world of sin." Now, there is a class of people who don't like this part of the Spirit's work. Do you know why? Because He convicts *them* of sin; they don't like that. What they want is someone to speak comforting words and make everything pleasant; keep everything all quiet; tell them there is peace when there is war; tell them it is light where it is dark; and tell them everything is growing better all the time. That is the kind of preaching they seek. Men think they are a great deal better than their fathers were. That suits human nature, for it is full of pride. Men will strut around and say, "Yes, I believe that; the world is improving; I am a much better man than father was. My father was too strict; he was one of those old Puritanical men who were so rigid. Oh, we are better than our fathers; we are getting on; we are more liberal; we will trample the laws of God under our feet."

That is the kind of preaching some dearly love, and there are preachers who tickle such itching ears. When you bring the Word of God to bear upon them, and when the Spirit drives it home, then men will say: "I don't like that kind of preaching; I will never go to hear that man again." Sometimes they will get up and stamp their way out of church before the speaker gets through; they don't like it. But when the Spirit of God is at work, He convicts men of sin. "When He has come, He will convict the world of sin, of righteousness, and of judgment: of sin"—not because men swear and lie and steal and get drunk and murder—"of sin, because they believe not in Me" (John 16:8–9).

THE CLIMAX SIN

That is the sin of the world. Why, a great many people think that unbelief is a sort of misfortune. They do not know, if you will allow me the expression, it is the damning sin of the world today; that is what unbelief is, the mother of all sin. There would not be a drunkard walking the streets, if it were not for unbelief; there would not be a harlot walking the streets, if it were not for unbelief; there would not be a murderer, if it was not for unbelief. It is the germ of all sin. Don't think for a moment that it is a misfortune, but just bear in mind it is an awful sin, and may the Holy Spirit convict every reader that unbelief is making God a liar. Many a man has been knocked down on the streets because someone has told him he was a liar. Unbelief is giving God the lie; that is the plain English of it.

Some people seem to boast of their unbelief; they seem to think it is quite respectable to be an infidel and doubt God's Word, and they will vainly boast and say, "I have intellectual difficulties; I can't believe." Oh, that the Spirit of God may come and convict men of sin! That is what we need—His convicting power, but I am so thankful that God has not put that into our hands. We have not to convict men; if we had, I would get discouraged, and give up preaching and go back to business within the next forty-eight hours. It is my work to preach and hold up the Cross and testify of Christ; but it is His work to convict men of sin and lead them to Christ. One thing I have noticed, that some conversions don't amount to anything; that if a man professes to be converted without conviction of sin, he is one of those stony-ground hearers who don't bring forth much fruit. The first little wave of persecution, the first breath of opposition, and the man is back in the world again.

Let us pray, dear Christian reader, that God may carry on a deep and thorough work, that men may be convicted of sin so that they cannot rest in unbelief. Let us pray God it may be a thorough work in the land. I would much rather see a hundred men thoroughly converted, truly born of God, than to see a thousand professed conversions where the Spirit of God has not convicted of sin. Don't go to the man who is living in sin, and tell him all he has to do is to stand right up and profess, without any hatred for sin. Let us ask God first to show every person the plague of his own heart, that the Spirit may convict of sin. Then will the work in our hands be real, and deep, and abide the fiery trial that will try everyone's labor.

Thus far, we have found the work of the Spirit is to impart life, to implant hope, to give liberty, to testify of Christ, to guide us into all truth, to teach us all things, to comfort the believers, and to convict the world of sin.

Ye are not your own." "Your bodies are the temples of the Holy Ghost." Is that an unmeaning metaphor, or an over-worded expression? When the Holy Spirit enters the soul, heaven enters with Him. The heart is compared to a temple. God never enters without His attendants; repentance cleanses the house; faith provides for the house; watchfulness, like the porter, takes care of it; prayer is a lively messenger, learns what is wanted, and then goes for it; faith tells him where to go, and he never goes in vain; joy is the musician of this temple, tuning to the praises of God and the Lamb; and this terrestrial temple shall be removed to the celestial world, for the trumpet shall sound, and the dead shall be raised.

—Rowland Hill

CHAPTER FOUR

POWER IN OPERATION

THE POWER WE HAVE BEEN CONSIDERING is the presence of the Holy Spirit. He is omnipotent. Power in operation is the actions of the Spirit or the fruit of the Spirit. This we shall now consider. Paul writes in Galatians 5:16–18, 22–26:

> I say then: Walk in the Spirit, and you shall not fulfill the lust of the flesh. For the flesh lusts against the Spirit, and the Spirit against the flesh; and these are contrary to one another, so that you do not do the things that you wish. But if you are led by the Spirit, you are not under the law. But the fruit of the Spirit is love, joy, peace, longsuffering, kindness, goodness,

faithfulness, gentleness, self-control. Against such there is no law. And those who are Christ's have crucified the flesh with its passions and desires. If we live in the Spirit, let us also walk in the Spirit. Let us not become conceited, provoking one another, envying one another.

Now there is a life of perfect peace, perfect joy, and perfect love, and that ought to be the aim of every child of God. That ought to be our standard, and we should not rest until we have attained to that position. That is God's standard, where He wants all His children. These nine graces mentioned in Galatians 5 can be divided in this way: Love and joy and peace are all to God. God looks for that fruit from each one of His children, and that is the kind of fruit which is acceptable with Him. Without that we cannot please God. He wants, above everything else that we possess, love, peace and joy. And then the next three—longsuffering, kindness, and goodness—are toward man. That is our outward life to those that we are coming in contact with continually—daily, hourly. The next three—faithfulness, gentleness, self-control—are in relation to ourselves.

LOVE, JOY, AND PEACE

The first thing that meets us as we enter the kingdom of God, you might say, are these first three graces: love, joy, and peace. When a man who has been living in sin turns from his sins, and turns to God with all his heart, he is met on the threshold of the divine life by these sister graces. The love of God is shed abroad in his heart by the Holy Spirit. The joy of the Lord comes at the same time, and also the peace of God. We can all put the test to ourselves, if we have them. It is not anything that we can make. The great trouble with many is that they are trying to make these graces. They are trying to make love; they are trying to make joy; they are trying to make peace. But they are not creatures of human planting. To produce them of ourselves is impossible. That is an act of God. They come from above. It is God who speaks the word and gives the love; it is God who gives the peace; it is God who gives the joy. And we possess all by receiving Jesus Christ by faith into the heart; for when Christ comes by faith into the heart, then the Spirit is there, and if we have the Spirit, we will have the fruit.

If the whole church of God could live as the Lord would have them live, Christianity would be the mightiest power this world has ever seen. It is the low standard of Christian life that is causing so much trouble. There are a great many stunted Christians in the church; their lives are stunted. They are like a tree planted in poor soil—the soil is hard and stony, and the roots cannot find the rich loamy soil needed. Such believers have not grown in these sweet graces. Peter described them this way:

> But also for this very reason, giving all diligence, add to your faith virtue, to virtue knowledge, to knowledge self-control, to self-control perseverance, to perseverance godliness, to godliness brotherly kindness, and to brotherly kindness love. For if these things are yours and abound, you will be neither barren nor unfruitful in the knowledge of our Lord Jesus Christ. (2 Peter 1:5–8)

Now, if we have these things in us, I believe that we will be constantly bringing forth fruit that will be acceptable with God. It won't be just a little every now and then, when we spur ourselves up and work ourselves up into a certain state of mind or into an excited condition, and work a little while and then become cold, and discouraged, and disheartened, but we will bring forth fruit constantly and will grow in grace and be filled with the Spirit of God.

WHAT WINS

A great many parents have inquired of me how to win their children. They say they have talked with them, and sometimes they have scolded them and have lectured them, and signally failed. I think there is no way so sure to win our families and our neighbors, and those about whom we are anxious, to Christ, than just to adorn the doctrine of Jesus Christ in our lives, and grow in all these graces. If we have peace and joy and love and gentleness and goodness and self-control, if we just live in our homes as the Lord would have us, with an even Christian life day by day, we shall have a quiet and silent power proceeding from us—a power that will constrain them to believe on the Lord Jesus Christ. But an uneven life, hot today and cold tomorrow, will only repel.

Many are watching God's people. It is just the very worst thing that can happen to those whom we want to win to Christ, to see us, at any time, in a cold, backslidden state. This is not the normal condition of the church; it is not God's intention; He would have us growing in all these graces, and the only true, happy, Christian life is to be growing, constantly growing in the love and favor of God, growing in all those delightful graces of the Spirit.

Even the vilest and most impure acknowledge the power of goodness; they recognize the fruit of the Spirit. It may condemn their lives and cause them to say bitter things at times, but down deep in their hearts they know that the man or woman who is living that kind of life is superior to them. The world doesn't satisfy them, and if we can show the world that Jesus Christ does satisfy us in our present life, it will be more powerful than the eloquent words of professional reformers. A man may preach with the eloquence of an angel, but if he doesn't live what he preaches, and act out in his home and his business what he professes, his testimony goes for naught, and the people say it is all hypocrisy after all; it is all a sham. Words are very empty if there is nothing back of them. Your testimony is worthless if there is not a record consistent with what you profess.

What we need is to pray to God to lift us up out of this low, cold state that we have been living in, that we may live in the atmosphere of God continually, and that the Lord may lift upon us the light of His countenance, and that we may shine in this world, reflecting His grace and glory.

The first of the graces spoken of in Galatians, and the last mentioned in Peter, is love. We cannot serve God unless we have love. It's the key that unlocks the human heart. If a mother shows by her actions that it is pure love that prompts her advising her boy to lead a different life, not a selfish love, but that it is for the glory of God, it won't be long before that mother's influence will be felt by that boy, and he will begin to think about this matter. True love touches the heart quicker than anything else.

THE POWER OF LOVE

Love is the badge that Christ gave His disciples. Some put on one sort of badge and some another. Some put on a strange kind of dress, that they may be known as Christians, and some put on a crucifix, or something else, that they may be known as Christians. But love is the only badge by which the disciples of our Lord Jesus Christ are known. "By this all will know that you are My disciples, if you have love for one another" (John 13:35).

Therefore, though a man stand before an audience and speak with the eloquence of a Demosthenes or of the greatest living orator, if there is no love back of his words, it is like sounding brass and a clanging cymbal. I would recommend all Christians to read 1 Corinthians 13 constantly, abiding in it day and night, not spending a night or a day there, but just go in there and spend all our time—twelve months in the year. Then the power of Christ and Christianity would be felt as it never has been in the history of the world. See what the first two verses say: "Though I speak with the tongues of men and of angels, but have not love, I have become as sounding brass or a clanging cymbal. And though I have the gift of prophecy, and understand all mysteries and all knowledge, and though I have all faith, so that I could remove mountains, but have not love, I am nothing."

A great many are praying for faith; they want extraordinary faith; they want remarkable faith. They forget that love exceeds faith. The love spoken of in the above verses, is a fruit of the Spirit, the great motive power of life. What the church of God needs today is love—more love to God and more love to our fellow men. If we love God more, we will love our fellow men more. There is no doubt about that. I used to think that I should like to have lived in the days of the prophets; that I should like to have been one of the prophets, to prophesy, and to see the beauties of heaven and describe them to men. Now, as I understand the Scriptures, I would rather live in the thirteenth chapter of 1 Corinthians and have this love that Paul is speaking of—the love of God burning in my soul like an unquenchable flame—so that I may reach people and win them for heaven.

A man may have wonderful knowledge that may unravel the mysteries of the Bible, and yet be as cold as an icicle. He may preach like an angel, Paul says, "with the tongues of men and of angels," but if he has no love, it amounts to nothing. "And though I bestow all my goods to feed the poor"(v. 3)—a man may be very charitable, and give away all he has, but if it is not the love of God that prompts the gift, it will not be acceptable with God. "And though I give my body to be burned, but have not love, it profits me nothing" (v.4). A man may go to the stake for his principles; he may go to the stake for what he believes, but if it is not love to God that actuates him, it will not be acceptable to God.

LOVE'S WONDERFUL EFFECTS

Notice love's other effects. It "suffers long and is kind; . . . does not envy; . . . does not parade itself, is not puffed up; does not behave rudely, does not seek its own, is not provoked, thinks no evil" (vv. 4–5).

That's the work of love. It is not provoked. Now if a man has no love of God in his heart, how easy it is to become offended; perhaps with the church because some members of the church don't treat him just right, or some men of the church don't bow to him on the street, he takes offense, and that is the last you see of him. Love also is longsuffering. If I love the Lord Jesus Christ, these little things are not going to separate me from His people. They are like the dust in the balance. Nor will the cold, formal treatment of hypocrites in the church quench that love I have in my heart for Him.

If this love is in the heart, and the fire is burning on the altar, we will not be all the time finding fault with other people and criticizing what they have done.

CRITICS BEWARE

Love will rebuke evil, but will not rejoice in it. Love will be impatient of sin, but patient with the sinner (see vv. 6–7). To form the habit of finding fault constantly is very damaging to spiritual life; it is about the lowest and meanest position that a man can take. I never saw a man who was aiming to do the best work, who could not show improvement. I never addressed an audience that I didn't think I could have done better, and I have often upbraided myself that I had not done better; but to sit down and find fault with other people when we are doing nothing ourselves, not lifting our hands to save someone, is all wrong. It is the opposite of holy, patient, divine love.

Love is forbearance; and what we want is to get

this spirit of criticism and fault-finding out of the church and out of our hearts. Let each one of us live as if we had to answer for ourselves and not for the community at the last day. If we are living according to 1 Corinthians 13, we will not be all the time finding fault with other people. Remember, "Love suffers long and is kind."

If we don't love the church of God, I am afraid it won't do us much good. What we want, then, is to have love for Christ, to have love for His Word, and to have love for the church of God. When we have such love, and are living in that spirit, we will not be in the spirit of finding fault and working mischief.

AFTER LOVE, WHAT?

After love comes joy. It is the privilege, I believe, of every Christian to walk in the light, as God is in the light, and it is our privilege to be full of the joy of the Lord. We read that when Philip went down to Samaria and preached, there was great joy in the city. Why? Because they believed the glad tidings. And that is the natural order, joy in believing. The seventy "returned with joy" from preaching salvation in the name of Jesus Christ, saying, "Lord, even the demons are subject to us in Your name." The Lord seemed to correct them in this one thing when He said, "Do not rejoice in this, that the spirits are subject to you, but rather rejoice because your names are written in heaven" (Luke 10:17, 20). They had something to rejoice in now. God doesn't ask us to rejoice over nothing, but He gives us some ground for our joy.

What would you think of a man or woman who seemed very happy today and full of joy, and couldn't tell you what made him or her so? Suppose I should meet a man on the street, and he was so full of joy that he should get hold of both my hands and say, "Bless the Lord, I am so full of joy!"

"What makes you so full of joy?"

"Well, I don't know."

"You don't know?"

"No, I don't; but I am so joyful that I just want to get out of the flesh."

Would we not think such a person unreasonable? But there are a great many people who feel—who want to feel—that they are Christians before they are Christians; they want the Christian's experience before they become Christians; they want to have the joy of the Lord before they receive Jesus Christ. But this is not the Gospel order. He brings joy when He comes, and we cannot have joy apart from Him; there is no joy away from Him. He is the author of it, and we find our joy in Him.

Now, there are three kinds of joy. First, there is the joy of one's own salvation. I thought, when I first tasted that, it was the most delicious joy I had ever known, and that I could never get beyond it. But I found, afterward, there was something more joyful than that, namely, the joy of the salvation of others.

JOY IS UNSELFISH

Oh, the blessed privilege to be used of God to win a soul to Christ, and to see a man or woman being led out of bondage by some act of ours toward them. To think that God should condescend to allow us to be coworkers with Him. It is the highest honor we can wear. It surpasses the joy of our own salvation, this joy of seeing others saved. And then John said Christ had no greater joy than to see His disciples walking in the truth. Every person who has been the means of leading souls to Christ understands what that means. Young disciples, walk in the truth and you will have joy all the while.

I think there is a difference between happiness and joy. Happiness is caused by things that happen around me, and circumstances will mar it. But joy flows right on through trouble. Joy flows on through the dark; joy flows in the night as well as in the day. It flows all through persecution and opposition; it flows right along, for it is an unceasing fountain bubbling up in the heart. The Lord gives His people perpetual joy when they walk in obedience to Him.

This joy is fed by the divine Word of God. Jeremiah wrote: "Your words were found, and I ate them, and Your word was to me the joy and rejoicing of my heart; for I am called by Your name, O Lord" (15:16).

He consumed God's words, and what was the result? He said they were the joy and rejoicing of his heart. Now people should look for joy in the Word, and not in the world; they should look for the joy that the Scriptures furnish, and then go work in the vineyard; because a joy that doesn't send me out to someone else, a joy that doesn't impel me to go and help the poor drunkard, a joy that doesn't prompt me to visit the widow and the fatherless, a joy that doesn't cause me to go into the Sunday school or other Christian work, is not worth having, and is not from above. Indeed, a joy that does not constrain me to go and work for the Master is purely sentiment and not real joy.

JOY IN PERSECUTION

There is a third kind of joy, one that continues during persecution. "Blessed are you when men hate you, and when they exclude you, and revile you, and cast out your name as evil, for the Son of Man's sake. Rejoice in that day and leap for joy! For indeed your reward is great in heaven, for in like manner their fathers did to the prophets" (Luke 6:22–23).

Christians do not receive their reward down here. We have to go right against the current of the world. We may be unpopular, and we may go against many of our personal friends if we live godly in Christ Jesus. At the same time, if we are persecuted for the Master's sake, we will have this joy bubbling up. It just comes right up in our hearts all the while—a joy that is unceasing, that flows right on. The world cannot choke that fountain.

We have this joy if we serve Him. A man or woman is not fit to work for God who is cast down, because that Christian goes about work with a telltale face. "The joy of the Lord is your strength" (Nehemiah 8:10). What we need today is a joyful church. A joyful church will make inroads upon the works of Satan, and we will see the Gospel going down into dark lanes and dark alleys, and we will see the drunkards reached and the gamblers and the harlots come pressing into the kingdom of God. It is this carrying a sad countenance, with so many wrinkles on our brows, that retards Christianity. Oh, may there come great joy upon believers everywhere, that we may shout for joy and rejoice in God day and night.

A joyful church—let us pray for that, that the Lord may make us joyful, and when we have joy, then we will have success. And if we don't have the reward we think we should have here, let us constantly remember the rewarding time will come hereafter.

Someone has said that if you had asked men in Abraham's day who their great man was, they would have said Enoch and not Abraham. If you had asked in Moses' day who their great man was, they would not have said it was Moses; he was nothing, but it would have been Abraham. If you had asked in the days of Elijah or Daniel, it wouldn't have been Daniel or Elijah; neither was anything; but it would have been Moses. And in the days of Jesus Christ, if you had asked about John the Baptist or the apostles, you would have heard they were mean and contemptible in the sight of the world. They were looked upon with scorn and reproach; but see how mighty they have become. And so we will not be appreciated in our day, but we are to toil on and work on, possessing this joy all the while. And if we lack it, let us cry: "Restore to me the joy of Your salvation, and uphold me by Your generous Spirit. Then I will teach transgressors Your ways, and sinners shall be converted to You" (Psalm 51:12–13).

A JOY THAT REMAINS

Jesus said, "These things I have spoken to you, that My joy might remain in you, and that your joy may be full" (John 15:11). Later He said, "You now have sorrow; but I will see you again and your heart will rejoice, and your joy no one will take from you" (John 16:22).

I am so thankful that I have a joy that the world cannot rob me of; I have something that it is not in the power of man or demon to deprive me of—and that is the joy of the Lord. "No one will take it from you." In the second century, they brought a martyr before a king, and the king wanted him to recant and give up Christ and Christianity, but the man spurned the proposition.

"If you don't do it," the king said, "I will banish you."

The man smiled and answered, "You can't banish

me from Christ, for He says He will never leave me nor forsake me."

The king got angry, and said, "Well, I will confiscate your property and take it all from you."

And the man replied, "My treasures are laid up on high; you cannot get them."

The king became still more angry, and said, "I will kill you."

"Why," the man answered, "I have been dead forty years; I have been dead with Christ; dead to the world, and my life is hid with Christ in God, and you cannot touch it."

And so we can rejoice, because we are on resurrection ground, having risen with Christ. Let persecution and opposition come, we can rejoice continually, and remember that our reward is great, reserved for us unto the day when He who is our Life shall appear, and we shall appear with Him in glory.

THE SECRET OF PEACE

Remember, then, that love is power, and joy is power; but now I will call attention to another fruit of the Spirit, and this too is power—the grace of peace.

A great many people are trying to make peace. But that has already been done. God has not left it for us to do; all that we have to do is to enter into it. It is a condition, and instead of our trying to make peace and to work for peace, we want to cease all that, and sweetly enter into peace.

If I discover a man in the cellar complaining because there is no light there, and because it is cold and damp, I say, "My friend, come up out of the cellar. There is a good warm sun up here, a beautiful spring day, and it is warm, it is cheerful and light. Come up, and enjoy it." He replies, "Oh, no, sir; I am trying to see if I can make light down here. I am trying to work myself into a warm feeling." And there he is working away, and he has been at it for a whole week.

I can imagine my reader smiling; but you may be smiling at your own picture. For this is the condition of many whom I daily meet who are trying to do this very thing—they are trying to work themselves into peace and joyful feelings. Peace is a condition into which we enter; it is a state; and instead of our trying to make peace, let us believe what God's Word declares, that peace has already been made by the blood of the Cross. Christ has made peace for us, and now what He desires is that we believe it and enter into it.

Now, the only thing that can keep us from peace is sin. God turned the way of the wicked upside down. There is no peace for the wicked, says my God. The wicked are like the troubled sea that cannot rest, casting up filth and mire all the while; but peace with God by faith in Jesus Christ—peace through the knowledge of forgiven sin, is like a rock; the waters go dashing and surging past it, but it abides. When we find peace, we shall not find it on the ground of innate goodness. It comes from without ourselves, but into us.

In John 16:33a, we read: "These things I have spoken to you, that in Me you might have peace." "In Me you might have peace"—Jesus Christ is the author of peace. He procured peace. His Gospel is the gospel of peace. "I bring you good tidings of great joy which will be to all people. For there is born to you this day in the city of David a Savior," and then came that chorus from heaven, "Glory to God in the highest, and on earth peace, goodwill toward men!" (Luke 2:10–11, 14). He brought peace. "In the world you will have tribulation, but be of good cheer, I have overcome the world" (John 16:33b).

How true that in the world we have tribulations. Are you in tribulation? Are you in trouble? Are you in sorrow? Remember this is our lot. Paul had tribulation, and others shared in grief. Nor shall we be exempt from trial. But within, peace may reign undisturbed. If sorrow is our lot, peace is our legacy. Jesus gives peace; and do you know there is a good deal of difference between His peace and our peace? Anyone can disturb our peace, but they can't disturb His peace. That is the kind of peace He has left us. Nothing can offend those who trust in Christ.

NOT EASILY OFFENDED

In Psalm 119:165, we find "Great peace have they which love thy law: and nothing shall offend them" (KJV). The study of God's Word will secure peace. You take those Christians who are rooted and grounded in the Word of God, and you find they have great peace. But those who don't study their Bible, and don't know their Bible, are easily offended when some little trouble comes, or some little persecution. Their peace is all disturbed. Just a little breath of opposition, and their peace is all gone.

Sometimes I am amazed to see how little it takes to drive all peace and comfort from some people. Some slandering tongue will readily blast it. But if we have the peace of God, the world cannot take that from us. It cannot give it; it cannot destroy it. We have to get it from above the world; it is peace that Christ gives. "Great peace have they which love Thy law, and nothing shall offend them." Christ says, "Blessed is he who is not offended because of Me" (Matthew 11:6). Now, if you will notice, wherever there is a Bible-taught Christian, one who has the Bible well marked, and daily feeds upon the Word by prayerful meditation, he will not be easily offended.

Such are the people who are growing and working all the while. But it is these people who never open their Bibles, these people who never study the Scriptures, who become offended, and are wondering why they are having such a hard time. They are the persons who tell you that Christianity is not what it has been recommended to them; that they have found it was not all that we claim it to be. The real trouble is, they have not done as the Lord has told them to do. They have neglected the Word of God. If they had been studying the Word of God, they would not be in that condition. If they had been studying the Word of God, they would not have wandered these years away from God, living on the husks of the world. But they have neglected to care for the new life; they haven't fed it, and the poor soul, being starved, sinks into weakness and decay, and is easily stumbled or offended.

I met a man who confessed his soul had fed on nothing for forty years. "Well," said I, "that is pretty hard for the soul—giving it nothing to feed on."

And that man is but a type of thousands and tens of thousands today; their poor souls are starving. This body that we inhabit for a day, and then leave, we take good care of; we feed it three times a day, and we clothe it, and take care of it. By and by it is going into the grave to be eaten up by the worms; but the inner man, which is to live on and on, and on forever, is lean and starved.

SWEET WORDS

In Numbers 6:22–26, we read: "And the Lord spoke to Moses, saying: 'Speak to Aaron and unto his sons, saying, "This is the way you shall bless the children of Israel. Say to them: 'The Lord bless you and keep you. The Lord make His face shine upon you; and be gracious to you; the Lord lift up His countenance upon you, and give you peace.'"'"

I think these are about as sweet verses as we find in

the Old Testament. I marked them years ago in my Bible, and many times I have turned over and read them. "The Lord lift up His countenance upon you, and give you peace." They remind us of the loving words of Jesus to His troubled disciples, "Peace, be still." The Jewish salutation used to be, as a man went into a house, "Peace be upon this house," and as he left the house the host would say, "Go in peace."

Then again, in John 14:27, Jesus said: "Peace I leave with you, My peace I give unto you; not as the world gives do I give to you. Let not your heart be troubled, neither let it be afraid." This is the precious legacy of Jesus to all His followers. Every man, every woman, every child, who believes in Him may share in this portion. Christ has willed it to them, and His peace is theirs.

This then is our Lord's purpose and promise. "My peace I give to you." He gives it, and He will not take it away again: "Not as the world gives do I give to you." But you know, when some men make their wills and deed away their property, there are some sharp, shrewd lawyers who will get hold of that will and break it all to pieces; they will go into court and break the will, and the jury will set the will aside, and the money goes into another channel. Now this will that Christ has made, neither devil nor man can break it. He has promised to give us peace, and there are thousands of witnesses who can say: "I have my part of that legacy. I have peace; I came to Him for peace, and I got it. I came to Him in darkness; I came to Him in trouble and sorrow. I was passing under a deep cloud of affliction, and I came to Him and He said, 'Peace, be still.' And from that hour peace reigned in my soul."

Yes, many have proved His invitation true, "Come to Me, all you who labor and are heavy laden, and I will give you rest" (Matthew 11:28). They found rest when they came. He is the author of rest. He is the author of peace, and no power can break that will; yea, unbelief may question it, but Jesus Christ rose to execute His own will, and it is in vain for man to contest it. Infidels and skeptics may tell us that it is all a myth, and that there isn't anything in it, and yet the glorious tidings is ever repeated, "Peace on earth, goodwill to man," and the poor and needy, the sad and sorrowful, are made partakers of it.

So, my reader, you need not wait for peace any longer. All you have to do is to enter into it today. You need not try to make peace. It is a false idea; you cannot make it. Peace is already made by Jesus Christ, and is now declared unto you.

PEACE DECLARED

When France and England were at war, a French vessel had gone off on a long whaling voyage. When they came back, the crew were short of water, and being now near an English port, they wanted to get water; but they were afraid that they would be taken if they went into that port. Some people in the port saw them, saw their signal of distress, and sent word to them that they need not be afraid, for the war was over, and peace had been declared. But they couldn't make those sailors believe it, and they didn't dare to go into port, although they were out of water. But at last they made up their minds they had better go in and surrender up their cargo and surrender up their lives to their enemies than to perish at sea without water. When they got in, they found out that peace indeed had been declared and that what had been told them was true. So there are a great many people who don't believe the glad tidings that peace has been made.

Jesus Christ made peace on the cross. He satisfied the claims of the law; and this law that condemns you and me has been fulfilled by Jesus Christ. He has made peace, and now He wants us just to enjoy it, just to believe it. Nor is there a thing to hinder us from doing it, if we will. We can enter into that blessing now, and have perfect peace. The promise is: "You will keep him in perfect peace, whose mind is stayed on You, . . . Trust in the Lord forever, for in Yah, the Lord, is everlasting strength" (Isaiah 26:3–4).

Now, as long as our minds are stayed on our dear selves, we will never have peace. Some people think more of themselves than of all the rest of the world. It is self in the morning, self at noon, and self at night. It is self when they wake up, and self when they go to bed. All the time they are looking at themselves and thinking about themselves instead of "looking unto Jesus, the author and finisher of our faith" (Hebrews 12:2). Faith is an outward look. Faith does not look within; it looks without.

It is not what I think, nor what I feel, nor what I have done, but it is what Jesus Christ is and has done. So we should trust in Him who is our strength, and whose strength will never fail.

Every vain thought and idle word, and every wicked deed, is like so many drops to quench the Spirit of God. Some quench Him with the lust of the flesh; some quench Him with cares of the mind; some quench Him with long delays. . . [or] doing a thing when the Spirit saith not. The Spirit is often grieved before He be quenched.

—H. Smith

In times when vile men held the high places of the land, a roll of drums was employed to drown the martyr's voice, lest the testimony of truth from the scaffold should reach the ears of the people,—an illustration of how men deal with their own consciences, and seek to put to silence the truth-telling voice of the Holy Spirit.

—Arnot

CHAPTER FIVE

HINDERED POWER

ISRAEL, WE ARE TOLD, LIMITED the Holy One of Israel. They vexed and grieved the Holy Spirit, and rebelled against His authority, but there is a special sin against Him that we may profitably consider. The first description of it is in Matthew 12:22–29, 31–32:

> Then one was brought to Him who was demon-possessed, blind and mute; and He healed him, so that the blind and mute man both spoke and saw. And all the multitudes were amazed and said, 'Could this be the Son of David?' Now when the Pharisees heard it they said, "This fellow does not cast out demons except by Beelzebub, the ruler of the demons."

But Jesus knew their thoughts, and said to them: "Every kingdom divided against itself is brought to desolation, and every city or house divided against itself will not stand. If Satan cast out Satan, he is divided against himself. How then will his kingdom stand? And if I cast out demons by Beelzebub, by whom do your sons cast them out? Therefore they shall be your judges. But if I cast out demons by the Spirit of God, surely the kingdom of God has come unto you. . . . Therefore I say to you, every sin and blasphemy will be forgiven men, but the blasphemy against the Spirit will not be forgiven men. Anyone who speaks a word against the Son of Man, it will be forgiven him; but whosoever speaks against the Holy Spirit, it will not be forgiven him, either in this age or in the age to come."

THE UNPARDONABLE SIN

That is Matthew's account of the sin against the Holy Spirit known as the unpardonable sin. Now let's read Mark's account: "When His own people heard about this, they went out to lay hold of Him, for they said, 'He is out of His mind.' And the scribes who came down from Jerusalem said, 'He has Beelzebub,' and 'By the ruler of the demons He casts out demons'" (3:21–22).

The word Beelzebub means *the Lord of filth.* They charged the Lord Jesus with being possessed not only with an evil spirit, but with a filthy spirit. Mark continued:

And He called them to Himself and said to them in parables, "How can Satan cast out Satan? If a kingdom is divided against itself, that kingdom cannot stand. And if a house is divided against itself, that house cannot stand. And if Satan has risen up against himself, and is divided, he cannot stand, but has an end. . . . Assuredly, I say to you, all sins will be forgiven the sons of men, and whatever blasphemies they may utter; but he who blasphemes against the Holy Spirit never has forgiveness, but is subject to eternal condemnation." (3:23–29)

Now, if it stopped there, we would be left perhaps in darkness, and we would not exactly understand what the sin against the Holy Spirit is; but the next verse throws light upon the whole matter. Observe, the verse reads: "Because they said, 'He has an unclean spirit'" (Mark 3:30).

I have met many atheists and skeptics and deists and infidels, both in this country and abroad, but I never met a man or woman who ever said that Jesus Christ was possessed of an unclean demon. I don't think you ever met such a person. I have heard men say bitter things against Christ, but I never heard any man stand up and say that he thought Jesus Christ was possessed with the devil, and that He cast out demons by the power of the devil. No man or woman has any right to say they have committed the unpardonable sin unless they have maliciously and willfully said that they believe that Jesus Christ had a devil in Him, and that He was under the power of the devil, and that He cast out devils by the power of the devil.

WHAT IT IS NOT

Because you perhaps have heard someone say that there is such a thing as grieving the Spirit of God, and resisting the Spirit of God until He has taken His flight and left you, you have said, "That is the unpardonable sin." It is not. I admit there is such a thing as resisting the Spirit of God, and resisting till the Spirit of God has departed; but if the Spirit of God has left any, they will not be troubled about their sins. The very fact that they are troubled, shows that the Spirit of God has not left them.

If a man is troubled about his sins, it is the work of the Spirit; for Satan never yet told him he was a sinner. Satan makes us believe that we are pretty good; that we are good enough without God, safe without Christ, and that we don't need salvation. But when a man wakes up to the fact that he is lost, that he is a sinner, that is the work of the Spirit. If the Spirit of God had left him, he would not be in that state; and just because men and women want to be Christians, is a sign that the Spirit of God is drawing them.

If resisting the Spirit of God is an unpardonable sin, then we have all committed it, and there is no hope for any of us; for I do not believe there is a minister, or a worker in Christ's vineyard, who has not sometime in his life resisted the Holy Spirit; who has not sometime in his life rejected the Spirit of God. To resist the Holy Spirit is one thing, and to commit that awful sin of blasphemy against the Holy Spirit, is another thing. We want to take the Scripture and just compare them.

BAD THOUGHTS

Now, some people say, "I have such blasphemous thoughts; there are some awful thoughts that come into my mind against God," and they think that is the unpardonable sin. We are not to blame for having bad thoughts come into our minds. If we harbor them, then we are to blame. But if the devil comes and darts an evil thought into my mind, and I say, "Lord, help me," sin is not reckoned to me. Who has not had evil thoughts flash into his mind, flash into his heart, and been called to fight them?

One old divine says, "You are not to blame for the birds that fly over your head, but if you allow them to come down and make a nest in your hair, then you are to blame. You are to blame if you don't fight them off." And so with these evil thoughts that come flashing into our minds: We have to fight them. We are not to harbor them; we are not to entertain them. If evil thoughts come into my mind, and evil desires, it is no sign that I have committed the unpardonable sin. If I love those thoughts and harbor them, and think evil of God, and think Jesus Christ a blasphemer, I am responsible for such gross iniquity; but if I charge Him with being the prince of devils, then I am committing the unpardonable sin.

Let us now consider the sin of grieving the Spirit. Resisting the Holy Spirit is one thing; grieving Him is another. Stephen charged the unbelieving Jews, "You always resist the Holy Spirit; as your fathers did, so do you" (Acts 7:51). The world has always been resisting the Spirit of God in all ages. That is the history of the world. The world is today resisting the Holy Spirit.

"Faithful are the wounds of a friend" (Proverbs 27:6a). The divine Spirit as a friend reveals to this poor world its faults, and the world only hates Him for it. He shows them the plague of their hearts. He convinces or convicts them of sin, therefore they fight the Spirit of God. I believe there is many a man resisting the Holy Spirit; I believe there is many a man today fighting against the Spirit of God.

So what is grieving the Spirit? In Ephesians 4:30–31, we read:

> And do not grieve the Holy Spirit of God, by whom you were sealed for the day of redemption. Let all bitterness, wrath, anger, clamor, and evil speaking be put away from you, with all malice. And be kind to one another, tenderhearted, forgiving one another, even as God in Christ forgave you.

Now, that was written to the church at Ephesus. I

believe today the church all over Christendom is guilty of grieving the Holy Spirit. Many believers in different churches wonder why the work of God is not revived. I think that if we search, we will find something in the church grieving the Spirit of God. It may be a mere schism in the church; it may be some unsound doctrine; it may be some division in the church.

HOW THE CHURCH GRIEVES THE SPIRIT

There is one thing I have noticed as I have traveled in different countries: I never yet have known the Spirit of God to work where the Lord's people were divided. Unity is one thing we must have if we are to have the Holy Spirit of God to work in our midst. If a church is divided, the members should immediately seek unity. Let the believers come together and get the difficulty out of the way. If the minister of a church cannot unite the people, if those that were dissatisfied will not fall in, it would be better for that minister to retire.

A good many ministers in this country are losing their time—some of them have lost months and years— seeing no fruit. And they will not see any fruit, because they have a divided church. Such a church cannot grow in divine things. The Spirit of God doesn't work where there is division. What we want today is the spirit of unity among God's children, so that the Lord may work.

Another thing that grieves the Spirit in the

churches is the miserable policy of introducing questionable entertainments. There are the lotteries, for instance, that we have in many churches. If a man wants to gamble, he doesn't have to go to some gambling den; he can stay in the church. And there are fairs—bazaars, as they call them—where they have raffles and grab bags. And if he wants to see a drama, he doesn't need to go to the theater, for many of our churches are turned into theaters; he may stay right in the church and witness the acting. I believe all these things grieve the Spirit of God. I believe when we bring the church down to the level of the world to reach the world, we are losing all the while and grieving the Spirit of God.

But some say if we take the standard and lift it up high, it will drive away a great many members from our churches. I believe it, and I think the quicker they are gone, the better. The world has come into the church like a flood, and how often you find an ungodly choir employed to do the singing for the whole congregation; the idea that we need an ungodly man to sing praises to God! It was not long ago I heard of a church where they had an unconverted choir, and the minister saw something about the choir that he didn't like, and he spoke to the chorister, but the chorister replied: "You attend to your end of the church, and I will attend to mine." You cannot expect the Spirit of God to work in a church in such a state as that.

The trouble is that we have let down the standard;

we have grieved the Spirit of God. One movement of God's power is worth more than all our artificial power, and what the church of God wants today is to get down in the dust of humiliation and confession of sin, and go out and be separated from the world; and then see if we do not have power with God and with man.

WHAT IS SUCCESS?

The Gospel has not lost its power; it is just as powerful today as it ever has been. We don't want any new doctrine. It is still the old Gospel with the old power—the Holy Spirit power—and if the churches will but confess their sins and put them away, and lift the standard instead of pulling it down, and pray to God to lift us all up into a higher and holier life, then the fear of the Lord will come upon the people around us.

When Jacob put away strange gods and set his face toward Bethel, the fear of God fell upon the nations around. And when the churches turn toward God, and we cease grieving the Spirit so that He may work through us, we will then have conversions all the while. Believers will be added to the church daily. It is sad when you look over Christendom and see how little spiritual power there is in the church of God today. Many of the church members do not even want this Holy Spirit power. They don't desire it; they want intellectual power; they want to get some man who will just draw a crowd, not caring whether anyone is saved. With them that is not the question. Only fill the pews, have good society, fashionable people. If the minister will only lecture and entertain, that would suit them.

I said to a man some time ago, "How are you getting on at your church?"

"Oh, splendid."

"Many conversions?"

"Well . . . well, on that side we are not getting on so well," he said. "But, we rented all our pews and are able to pay all our running expenses; we are getting on splendidly."

That is what the godless call "getting on splendidly," because they rent the pews, pay the minister, and pay all the running expenses. Conversions! That is a strange thing.

There was a man being shown through one of the cathedrals of Europe; he had come in from the country, and one of the men belonging to the cathedral was showing him around, when he inquired, "Do you have many conversions here?"

"Many what?"

"Many conversions here?"

"Ah, man, this is not a Wesleyan chapel."

The idea of there being conversions there! And you can go into a good many churches in this country and ask if they have many conversions there, and they would not know what it meant, they are so far away from the Lord. They are not looking for conversions and don't expect them.

SHIPWRECKS

Alas, how many young converts have made shipwreck against such churches! Instead of being a harbor of delight to them, they have proved false lights, luring them to destruction. Isn't it time for us to get down on our faces before God and cry mightily to Him to forgive us our sins? The quicker we own it, the better. You may be invited to a party, and it may be made up of church members, and what will be the conversation? Oh, I got so sick of such parties that I left years ago. I would not think of spending a night that way. It is a waste of time; there is hardly a chance to say a word for the Master. If you talk of a personal Christ, your company becomes offensive. They don't like it; they want you to talk about the world, about a popular minister, a popular church, a good organ, a good choir. They say, "Oh, we have a grand organ, and a superb choir," and all that, and it suits them; but that doesn't warm the Christian heart. When you speak of a risen Christ and a personal Savior, they don't like it.

The fact is, the world has come into the church and taken possession of it, and what we want to do is to wake up and ask God to forgive us for "grieving the Spirit."

Dear reader, search your heart and inquire, "Have I done anything to grieve the Spirit of God?" If you have, may God show it to you today; if you have done anything to grieve the Spirit of God, you want to know it today, and get down on your face before God and ask Him to forgive you and help you to put it away. I have lived long enough to know that if I cannot have the power of the Spirit of God on me to help me to work for Him, I would rather die, than live just for the sake of living. How many are there in the church today, who have been members for fifteen or twenty years, but have never done a solitary thing for Jesus Christ? They cannot lay their hands upon one solitary soul who has been blessed through their influence; they cannot point today to one single person who has ever been lifted up by them.

QUENCHING THE SPIRIT

In 1 Thessalonians 5:19, we are told not to quench the Spirit. Now, I am confident the cares of the world are coming in and quenching the Spirit for a great many. They say, "I don't care for the world"; perhaps not the *pleasures* of the world so much after all as the *cares* of this life; but they have just let the cares come in and quench the Spirit of God. Anything that comes between me and God—between my soul and God—quenches the Spirit.

It may be my family. You may say: "Is there any danger of my loving my family too much?" Not if we love God more; but God must have the first place. If I love my family more than God, then I am quenching the Spirit of God within me. If I love wealth, if I love fame, if I love honor, if I love position, if I love pleasure, if I love self more than I love God who created and saved me—then I am committing a sin; I am not only grieving the Spirit of God, but quenching Him, and robbing my soul of His power.

THE EMBLEMS OF THE SPIRIT

But I would further call attention to the emblems of the Holy Spirit. An emblem is something that represents an object; the same as a balance is an emblem of justice, and a crown an emblem of royalty, and a scepter is an emblem of power; so we find in Exodus 17:6 that water is an emblem of the Holy Spirit. You find in the smitten rock, in the wilderness, the work of the Trinity illustrated. "'Behold, I will stand before you there on the rock in Horeb; and you shall strike the rock, and water will come out of it, that the people may drink.' And Moses did so in the sight of the elders of Israel."

In 1 Corinthians 10:4, Paul declared that the rock was Christ; it represented Christ. God says: "I will stand upon the rock," and as Moses smote the rock the water came out, which was an emblem of the Holy Spirit. It flowed out along through the camp, and they drank of the water. Now water is cleansing; it is fertilizing; it is refreshing; it is abundant, and it is freely given. So the Spirit of God does the same cleansing, fertilizing, refreshing, reviving, and He was freely given when the smitten Christ was glorified.

Then, too, fire is an emblem of the Spirit. It is

purifying, illuminating, searching. We talk about searching our hearts. We cannot do it. What we want is to
have God search them. Oh, that God may search us
and bring out the hidden things, the secret things that
cluster there and bring them to light.

The wind is another emblem. It is independent,
powerful, sensible in its effects. It is reviving; how the
Spirit of God revives when He comes to all the droop-
ing members of the church.

Then the rain and the dew: fertilizing, refreshing,
abundant. And there's the dove, gentle—what more
gentle than the dove? There's the lamb, gentle, meek,
innocent—a sacrifice. We read of the wrath of God;
we read of the wrath of the Lamb; but nowhere do we
read of the wrath of the Holy Spirit—gentle, innocent, meek, loving. It's that Spirit who wants to take
possession of our hearts. And He comes as a voice—
another emblem—speaking, guiding, warning, teaching. He is the seal: impressing, securing, and making
us as His own.

May we know Him in all His wealth of blessing.
This is my prayer for myself—for you. May we heed
the words of the grand apostle in 1 Corinthians 2:4–5:
"My speech and my preaching were not with persua-
sive words of human wisdom, but in demonstration of
the Spirit, and of power, that your faith should not be
in the wisdom of men but in the power of God."

More Quality Life Essentials Books

What Every Christian Should Believe

Getting grounded in the essentials of the faith is the key to a deep, abiding relationship with Christ. *What Every Christian Should Believe* is a classic primer on the basics of the Christian faith. Whether you're a new believer needing a primer on the basics of Christianity or a seasoned Christian desiring a comprehensive refresher, this book is a timeless classic to prepare you for today's Christian walk.

ISBN #0-8024-5220-5, Paperback

Experiencing Pleasure and Profit in Bible Study

Dwight L. Moody recognized the common struggle people have to regularly and thoroughly study the Bible. Knowing God's Word is essential for you to have a vibrant, growing Christian life. This classic work, refreshed and updated, will renew your enthusiasm to discover the life-changing truths contained in the precious Word of God.

ISBN #0-8024-5222-1, Paperback

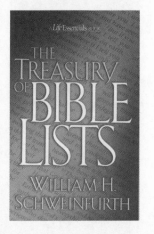

The Treasury of Bible Lists

The Treasury of Bible Lists is a rich compilation of Bible truths. They are designed to equip you to do in-depth study of a topic in Scripture, prepare presentations, or meditate upon a multitude of principles within Christianity.

ISBN #0-8024-5221-3, Paperback

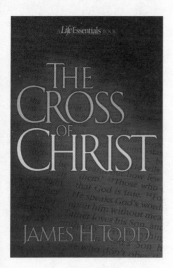

Cross of Christ

If you look closely at the Cross of Christ you will see, pain, humiliation, and death. But take a closer look and you will see ultimate love, redemption for sinners, the eternal plan of God for mankind, and His motivation to serve God the Father. James Todd surveys the Cross of Christ and sees all this and more. Learn about such terms as propitiation, atonement, and substitution, and what they mean for your present comfort and future hope.

ISBN #0-8024-5216-7, Paperback

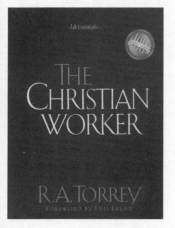

The Christian Worker

With a proper focus on the Word of God and the power of the Holy Spirit, this volume covers a variety of topics, including the basics of the gospel, one-on-one work and evangelistic meetings, preparing a sermon, and counseling unbelievers and straying Christians. Using Scripture passages to answer unbelievers' questions, objections and excuses, *The Christian Worker* is a useful book for those who have been doing evangelism for years or for those who are new to the experience.

ISBN #0-8024-5218-3, Paperback